M000308593

# My Name is Shield Woman

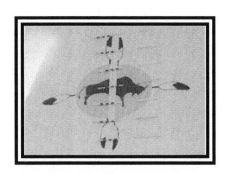

a hard road to healing, vision, and leadership

## Ruth Awo Taanaakii Scalp Lock

with Jim Pritchard

Dear Katherine

Thanks for your
support / understanding.
Love all my relations
God Bless!

Ruth Scalp Lock.

This story is dedicated to the survivors of the residential schools, and to our youth, for the healing of the past, our work in the present, and our prayers for the future.

# Forward

## Mildred Broad Scalplock

I met Ruth Scalp Lock in 1978 after the birth of my second child, Dallas Scalplock. I was married to Ruth Scalp Lock's nephew, Delbert Scalplock for 21 years in which we had four children together; my eldest son, Quinton, Dallas, Del and Mardi, our daughter. My sons played competitive sports in hockey and son Del in the pro rodeo circuit in the boy's steer riding event. Ruth fell in love with both sports. She was very active in her nephews' sports activities. Ruth also managed the Siksika Senior Men's Hockey Club. She fundraised, donated funds and volunteered her time to the club. She enjoyed and had fun doing what she loved.

Ruth loves the sport of chuck wagon racing. She never misses the annual Calgary Stampede Rangeland Derby of Chuck wagon racing. Ruth is very supportive of her nephew, Shawn Calf Robe, who is a world class outrider. Ruth is a proud and a devoted fan of Shawn.

Ruth also supported my daughter, Mardi in her pursuit in completing her post-secondary education by providing her with an educational tool called the I Pad and a Pendleton blanket for cuddling during those tough times as student in a city unknown to her. Ruth has always been an intricate part of our family. She expressed her support and deep love to my children and my 10 grand-children, who admire her, respect her and my grandchildren call her Grama. My son, Dallas affectionately nicknames her Ruthless. We love Ruth because she loves us and takes loving care of us. This includes her own children; Karleen Stone Child (daughter), Trevor Stone Child (son), Melton Paddy Scalplock (deceased son), grand-children; Chantel Stone Child, Shawn Scalplock, Dana Stone Child, Carlon One Spot, Faith Mills, Jacoby Marroone, Great-grandchildren; Samarah Scalplock, Jaiza Scalplock, Josh Scalplock and Nolan Scalplock and numerous nieces and nephews; includes her adopted children; Bernie Bear Hat, Maury Ayoungman and her adopted family the Weasel Child Family. We treasure her.

Ruth is a fun loving, crazy and free spirited woman who engages in a good laugh! I scream, she screams louder, along with her outburst of laughter, with a sexy hiccup and yow at the end of her laugh. She has an infectious laugh!

I remembered one time we organized a barbeque event for our clientele of Siksika women. Someone decided to plant what looked like a black substance or gun powder in the barbeque stove prior to our event. After the rocks were hot and some of the steaks were placed on the grill, there was a loud explosion from the barbeque stove. Women ran in every direction and steaks were flying all over the place. I saw Mavis our Elder run into the bushes and trees and Ruth running towards our office. They were fast. Ruth sprinted 100 feet in a matter of 3 seconds. I have never witnessed a person run so fast in high heels with steaks on both hands. We had a good laugh! We collected the steaks that fell on the ground. We brushed the debris and dirt off the steaks and grilled them to perfection. I think the foreign substances enhanced the flavor to our steaks.

Ruth used to work as a family support worker under the Siksika Child Welfare Services, before she became our Tribal Council member. A classy woman, Ruth is very fashionable, great taste in her wardrobe. I remember one time she came into the training room where 20 young adult males and females were gathered to start the workshop. Ruth came into the room very gracefully, smiling at everybody and saying her good morning to all, as she made her way to the coffee room. Everyone was giggling at Ruth and whispering when she passed by them. I looked at Ruth as she passed me and I gasped; yaw, the back of her skirt was up to her waist covered over by her pantyhose. I ran and shooed her out the door and whispered to her that she was not totally covered and her underwear is showing white. She screamed and laughed; she was embarrassed red, but never a person to be shamed she took all into stride. The students did not carry on about what happened to her; as they admired and had a great respect for her, their Coach.

Ruth is a beautiful Blackfoot Cree woman with a heart of gold and compassion for people that crossed her path. A lot of people have experienced her benevolence in helping them out in their predicament. Ruth is invigorating in her compassion to help people. She has been admired for her dedication and support to Native women who find themselves in domestic violence and in drugs and alcohol. This was evident in her initiative and work in the conception of the Native Women Shelter in the city of Calgary, named after her, Awo Taan. Ruth experienced her own journey in the world of addictions and domestic violence. We women who have come from the similar experience can relate to her story. Ruth's story will give hope and encouragement to women who may still be going through horrendous experiences with addictions and domestic violence.

Ruth, she is my comfort and joy. A long time friend of mine...

Kinanaskomitinawew, Thank-you (Cree)
Nitsiniiyi'taki (nehd-seh-nee-yeh'dahgi) Thank you (Blackfoot)

# Preface

## Jim Pritchard

This is a story that I am honoured to help tell.

Ruth Scalp Lock is a Siksika woman whom I have known for more than thirty years, first meeting at a downtown Child Welfare Office in Calgary. I have always had great respect and affection for Ruth, and that has only grown over the years. Maybe it took that long to put the pieces together and get the scope of her whole story, and what it means. That it is why one day I asked her if anyone had ever written about her. The answer was a humble "No," and I said that someone should, and I would try to help do that.

So the stories began. We spent hours together recounting the journey, the struggles, and ultimately, not only survival, but the emergence of a visionary, a teacher, a healer, and a leader - one who has touched many. Ruth is one who is never deterred by those who would say, "It can't be done," or to be overwhelmed by the stress and challenges of the moment. She will not absorb the bad energies, fending them off, and moving forward on her path, relentlessly.

This is a gritty story- the hard times are not glossed over. But it is one that is ultimately colored by Ruth's grace and humor, no doubt key to her survival, her strength, and her relationships. In the telling of this story, there were many tears, and just as much laughter.

This is first a story of one woman, an Aboriginal woman. It is also a story of the Aboriginal People, their struggles and perseverance.

This is also the story of many others that you will hear from. These are the people who worked with Ruth and helped her along the way. Some of these the reader will recognize. Others are not so well known, but are huge in their role in walking with Ruth. This is a salute to them as well, those who are committed to making their difference.

There are also those who tried to stop Ruth, and they too need to be recognized, for they also helped her on her way.

I want to make a few comments on the writing of this book. Overall, we have attempted to retain the authentic voice of Ruth, so the reader can get a sense of her as a real person, her "voice." In some cases, we have included Blackfoot words, using a particular spelling, which may vary from other variations, such as translation is. Ruth will refer to her people variously as Indian, Native, or Aboriginal. This reflects the historical trends. Many times in our conversations over the years she has used the term Indian, "I am proud to be an Indian." Lastly, Ruth will refer to the Creator, Jesus and the Holy Spirit. Some will find this confusing. She does not. For Ruth, there is One.

A huge part of Ruth is her commitment to reach out to people, to learn about them, and to teach them the ways of her people. One night, with my wife and children, I attended a naming ceremony where there were many white people at the gathering. The Elder, Eve Yellow Old Woman, looked out, and said, "It's amazing, never before, all these white people here tonight." We felt welcome, and there was one reason we were there - Ruth, through our long roads together, had brought us to this place.

This is a story of hope. It is a path to a healed world, a more equal one, and a more understanding one.

# Introduction and Acknowledgements

## Ruth Scalp Lock

I am sharing my life story to help other survivors of the residential schools, and the effects it had on their lives, to help them deal with what they went through – some horrific experiences. A person can change, once you come to terms with yourself and your experience. There is a way out.

I also want to help educate society. I personally want people to understand why First Nations People have so many problems to deal with. I want the young people – our youth – to know all that we went through.

This book is about what has happened to me, telling my experience and what I have learned. It is from my heart, the place where my People feel what is true and real.

I have been blessed to have so many good influential people in my life. They have helped me on my road and have been a source of strength and learning for me. I would like to acknowledge my husband and my children, my traditional adopted children and Grandchildren, and my step children. I thank the Creator who has given me many special Grandchildren and Great Grandchildren for me to enjoy and be part of my journey.

I thank my special adoptive mother Alice Weasel Child and family, Joe, Elden, Donna, Rose, Verna, Stephanie, and Elnora. I would also like to acknowledge my sister Marie Calf Robe and family, Eve Yellow Old Woman and family, and Veronica Smith and Family from the Piikani Reserve. I thank Robert Calf and Family and Allan Wolf Leg Sr. and Family, both who I grew up with on the Siksika Nation. Also

Bernard Tallman, Tracy Brass, Joyce First Rider, and Charlie Manyfires. I thank my adopted children, Iris, Terri and Nadine Grey Eyes, and also Clint Nelson.

Also I thank my adopted siblings, the Louis Family from the Hobbema Reserve, Wilda, Roy, and Del, as well as my adopted brother Austin Tootoosis from the Poundmaker Reserve in Saskatchewan. I also wish to thank Roger Running Crane, siblings and Family, from Browning Montana, and my very special nephews Shawn Calf Robe, Dallas, Quinton and Del Scalp Lock, Marlon and Tom Many Guns.

Madeline Dunkley was my Life Skills Coach in Edmonton, who believed and had faith in me, that I could make changes in my life. Today, I still use the skills she taught me many years ago. Also Flora Zaharia, my friend and support during my early time of recovery.

I want to express a deep appreciation and love for Nelson Gutnick who passed away in March 2014. He was my special teacher, mentor, guide, adviser, and friend. Thank you Nelson.

Jim Pritchard, my co-author, was very patient and understanding all these months, the endless hours we spent to get this book done. I always enjoy his sense of humour and taking the time to ask questions in so many different ways for me to be able to tell my story. Leroy Good Eagle Wolf Collar read the draft; it takes a special friend to be upfront and give honest feedback. I thank him for taking the time to read this and help us with this work.

I hope this story will be a learning tool for all walks of life. I am celebrating 40 years of sobriety on March 15, 2014. For that, first and foremost I give gratitude to the Creator, the one who made all of us and everything, for being in my heart every day. I give all the credit to the Creator who showed me the way. I embrace the Creator in my walk.

I hope you learn something from this story, and that our People find healing, and that all people find understanding for each other.

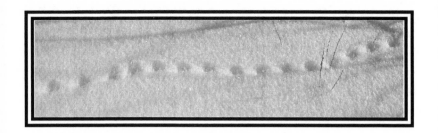

## The Gift

A long time ago, before Humans came to this world, the Creator held a Council with all of the Animals. The Creator said to them, I have a special Gift for the two-leggeds, the Humans, when they come to the Earth.

But they are not ready for this Gift of theirs,
It is too powerful.
They do not have the wisdom to understand how to use it.
They will hurt themselves, and Mother Earth.
So I don't want them to find it until they are ready.
We must hide it until then.

So the Buffalo said, give it to me and I will hide it in the long prairie grasses.
But the Creator said, no, the Humans will cut the grasses down and dig it up.

And the Bear said, give it to me and I will take the Gift to the mountains and hide it there, deep in the rock.
No, said the Creator, the Humans will make machines and tear down the mountains.

Then the Salmon said, I will hide the Gift in the waters of the oceans.
No, said the Creator, the Humans will go down deep and find it.

So, the Eagle came forward and said, I will take the Gift high into the

Sky beyond the stars.

No, said the Creator, the Humans will learn to fly and find it there.

The Creator asked again, where shall we hide this Gift until the Humans are ready? The Animals talked among themselves.

Then, a little mouse ran up onto the shoulder of the Creator and whispered in his ear.

The Creator smiled, and laughed. The Creator told the Council of Animals that he had found the answer and had learned important things. All of the powerful animals wanted to know who of the wise ones came up with the answer.

The Creator said, we need to listen to the little people in our lives, the ones who don't speak, whose voices are not heard. They have something important to listen to. We can learn so much from them.

And so, we will hide this Gift inside the Humans. They will never look there. Only when they are ready to use this Gift in a good way, will they know where to look, within themselves, in their own hearts.

# Part I

# Shaken Foundations

"We fell asleep to the old songs, and the familiar voices."

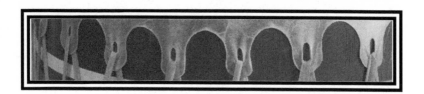

## Chapter 1 I still hear the holy songs

*March, 1974... It was a cold night. I was drunk and crazy. We were in an all-night restaurant in Winnipeg.*

*I looked over across at a white guy at a table. He was laughing...I thought he must be laughing at me. I didn't like it so I went over and grabbed him by the hair and threw him on the floor.*

*My friend said, "What are you doing!?" Someone called the cops.*

*We ran out the door and down the street. We ended up at the Winnipeg Hotel, very expensive. I don't know how we paid for it.*

*I drank everything I could find in the bar fridge all night long. I was lost in a miserable trance, passing out, waking up.*

*And then, in the middle of the night, the darkest hour, my life changed forever...*

Oki Napi. Hello my Friends. My name is Ruth Scalp Lock.

My Blackfoot name, given to me later in life, is Awo Taanaakii (a-woo-tan-a-kee). This is a powerful name, sacred to me, meaning Shield Woman, the Woman who carries the Shield to protect others from harm. Later in my story I will share the meaning of this name and how it came to me.

I was born September 25, 1944 at Gleichen, Alberta at the Blackfoot Hospital, an hour east of Calgary. Our Nation is Siksika (Seek-seek-ah).

As a child, I was taught that we are part of the Blackfoot People. We called ourselves, Niitsitapii, The Real People. Within the Blackfoot people, there is the Siksika (Blackfoot), the Piikani (Peigan), the Kainai (Blood), and the Blackfeet in Montana. In 1877, the Canadian Government signed Treaty 7 with the Blackfoot Confederacy, along with two other Nations, the Nakoda and Tsuu T'ina.

The Treaty is sacred to our people, the agreement between the white society and our Nations. At the time of the signing, the sacred medicine pipe was on the table, our traditional symbol for peace. Our Head Chief in the process was Chief Crowfoot. It is told among our People that the officials tried to get him drunk, and our medicine people saw this and removed him to be doctored back to health. These negotiations were too important. He came back to the table and told the negotiators the meaning of the Treaty to our People. He took the dollar bill, symbolizing money, and lit it, the ashes falling out of his hand. Then he picked up some earth in his hand, rubbing it between his fingers, "To my People, the money means nothing, it disappears. The Earth is the Creator's, it lasts forever." This is what happened. It is true.

The Treaty is an agreement to live in peace and share the land. This has been drilled into my head by the Elders. Our Siksika Coat of Arms has the colours yellow, green and blue. These circles represent the duration of the Treaty, as long as the sun shines, the grass grows, and the river flows. It was supposed to create equality for our people. It has not worked out that way for us.

I was so fortunate that as a young child I learned the old ways of my People. From as long as I remember, I learned the traditional cultural knowledge of our people from my Father and the Elders. I went to ceremonies as a child. I understood everything in Blackfoot.

There was no English. From the stories that were told to me, this area, based in Alberta, is our traditional territory. This area stretched from south of Edmonton, right into Yellowstone in the States. The Blackfoot People have always been known historically as leaders – great warriors – back then and today.

This is Napi's land, the Blackfoot's Old Man. He was known as a trickster, exploring the world. There are many sacred sites and signs of our people throughout this area. There is Okotoks, the Big Rock. There are others, tipi rocks, and effigies. Just south of our Nation, is the old, large Medicine Wheel. All these things signify that we have been here long before the written history.

The effigies are stones our People put in the ground, representing different shapes, many of a large man. This is Napi. They were able to communicate, to say that a certain family was here. Our ancestors were so smart to put those things in the ground, saying this is my clan, this is my area. There is one big effigy, up on the hill by the town of Cluny. One of the farmers there, it's right on his land.

I laugh when they say we are from Siberia. To me that's a joke. I grew up with the feeling that my people were here and this was their place, this was their home, even though I hear different people say that we came through the Bering Straight. I know maybe other Aboriginal or Native people believe it, but I certainly don't.

My late Father was Tom Scalp Lock, who was born here at Siksika in 1900. Then, this was known simply as the Blackfoot Reserve.

My mother was Flora Butterfly, who was from Maple Creek, Saskatchewan. Originally, she was born in Duck Lake. My mother was Cree, from the Beardy's Reserve. On my mother's side my ancestors were very nomadic. They moved down to Maple Creek, then Grandfather and family moved to Alberta. They moved to Medicine Hat, then to Bassano, twenty miles east of Crowfoot, which is where our Reserve starts. My Grandparents were camped there and became friends with people from Siksika. At that time the

Siksika adopted my Grandfather and the family. That is how they became members of Siksika.

My parents' marriage was arranged. My Father's and Mother's parents agreed for them to get married. So they were married and my mother stayed here. She never went back to see her family, but she always wanted to – she always told me that when I grew up I should make something of myself, have an education and a job and one day to have a vehicle, so that I could take her to visit her relatives in Maple Creek, Duck Lake, Poundmaker, Sweetgrass – all those reserves in Saskatchewan.

I never did get to drive my mother back to her home. She died May 9, 1963 when I was still at the residential school. My mother – even talking about it today still bothers me.

I always feel cheated because I never really got to know my mother's relatives. Here and there I got information or I found out who I'm related to. I know of some of those relatives – I had a first cousin who was a Chief for a long time, Gordon Oakes. Today I would have had two Native languages – Blackfoot and Cree. Because I was raised here, I learned the Blackfoot language and culture.

So I come from two clans, my Father's side which was the White Elk Clan, and my mother's side, which was the Cree Clan.

My Father's Mother was from Piikani, at Brocket in Southern Alberta, where we always went to visit. I'm very close to my late Dad's relatives at Brocket, as well as the Bloods. We always visited them and they would come and visit us. There would be a big celebration, a feast, or a pow wow, any kind of gathering.

My Father brought me to all the ceremonies as a child. I had my face painted, when I was young, before I went to the residential school. I had that foundation – a strong Siksika foundation, the culture and the language. My Father always wanted me to be there and I listened. My father was in all the religious Societies – the Horn

Society, the Prairie Chicken Society, the Brave Dog Society. My Father made a strong commitment to be in those Societies, and he really practised the traditional way, and the special rights he had as a member.

I remember. I can still hear the singing, the holy songs, and all the sacred things that took place. But those days will never come back for me. To be honest I'll never be in a society, because my way of healing is different. I have my own way of healing. A society is a religious society, and I really don't have the rights to talk about them, because it is sacred knowledge. They can really help a person to change and recover from things that have happened in their lives. It really changes their attitude, and their behaviour.

In Siksika we have the Horn Society today. Most of this very sacred Society was passed on by my parents' generation. The Horn Society is going to start camping down at the River here, with the new members of the Society. They camp and have their ceremonies, and then the public can come. The new people make a commitment to go, in the Summer, to speak to the Elders, and to get better. They have a special protocol that they have to follow when they approach the Elders to ask for their help.

I learned so much before I went to the residential school. I was told that I had a purpose in life. It was going to come and I would have to contribute to Siksika. My Father always told me "One day you're going to have children, you're going to have grandchildren – you treat your kids, and those grandchildren, very special, because they're gifts from the Creator." I still have that in the back of my mind today.

I grew up in the Cluny area of our Nation, where we homesteaded. Today I live not even half a mile from where I grew up. I learned how to work and helped my mother. She worked like a man – Holy, was she a woman! She never just sat in the house. In the winter time she would go down to the coal mines with somebody else, maybe with another woman or one of my brothers or myself. We would go down to the river, get blocks of ice, and we'd bring it home. My mother would thaw the blocks of ice. We used it for cooking, to drink, and to bath. Water was so pure back then. Water is a powerful thing, an important gift that cleanses ourselves and our souls. This River we have that flows through our land, the Bow River, is polluted now from the city upstream. But back then, it was so fresh, smelled so clean, and made your skin feel soft. To us, the water was like medicine.

I really enjoyed the way we lived, because I learned to work as a child. I think that's why today I refuse to retire. It was instilled in my mind to work.

I had many brothers and sisters, Paul, Glenter, Lawrence, Donald, Albert, Lucy, Rosemary, Marie, Frank Turning Robe Sr., and Jane Drunkenchief. That's why we had to work so hard! I always had hand-me-downs and we shopped at the Salvation Army. We just had a two-bedroom house. Some of us had beds and some of us slept on the floor.

I used to watch my mom cut wild meat. She would make dried meat and smoke it. In the summertime we would go berry picking. We'd come home and she would crush the chokecherries, dry the Saskatoon berries, and then she would store it all for the winter.

I learned all these good things – even to clean the house. My Father used to say we have to keep our home clean, this is our safe haven, even the outside. When Spring came, we had to clean the yard, because people will know what kind of person you are when they come to your home. But don't just look good on the outside, he would say. Look good on the inside of your home too. The inside of your home is like your heart, it has to be kept too.

My Father was a farmer. He farmed a section of land. But also, he worked with Louie Hong, who had a store in Cluny about a mile from where we lived. My Father worked hard - those were some of the good things I remember. He worked at the store for about 40 or 50 years. He was a jack of all trades, a clerk, a cleaner, a waiter, stacked the shelves. He did everything. I think he helped Louie to become a millionaire!

My Father didn't have perfect English. When he asked the customers at Hongs if they wanted dessert, it was always the same question, "What kind of apple pie do you want?"

That makes me smile still.

My Mother had gifts for healing. She had "medicine," but she never passed it on to us – maybe I was too young at the time and then I was at the residential school. I know she had those gifts for healing because I did see her heal a man who was dying.

I always used to put my Dad up on a pedestal. But when I started my healing journey, later in life when I quit drinking, all these things started to surface. As I became older and more aware, I used to ask my Mother, "What was he like to you?" My mom shared some stories with me.

There were some things that I was aware of then, not to the extent of me having to run out of the house and whatnot - but there was that underlying something that I knew. There were a few times I heard my dad call my mom some unpleasant things – her being Cree, this and that, put downs. But I guess it took time and it really helped him when he joined these Societies. I didn't see my dad physically hit my Mother but I always felt there was some kind of violence – because there were times I saw bruises, maybe on her arm or whatever, and sometimes she was afraid to say some things and those were indicators. I guess today I can see it.

These are some of the things I spoke to my Father about. But these things really bothered me. I needed to get more answers. Eventually he shared more with me – having to accept my Mother for who she was, because my Mother was a go-getter. She would do a lot of things on her own, just so we had food and whatever we needed.

My Dad said it took him time to love my Mother and for them to get to know each other. I asked him how they communicated, because neither spoke English, nor the same Native language. I guess it was all sign language. My Mother didn't even know a word of Blackfoot. But later on my Mother spoke fluent Blackfoot. She learned the language and she really got to know the Blackfoot culture.

My Dad died March 29, 1982. Before that, I asked my Dad, "Did you ever love my mother? How come these things happened?" I always suspected or felt that he didn't love my mother because it was an arranged marriage. He said, "I loved your mother."

After my mom passed away May 9, 1963 my Father never got into another relationship.

My Father was a strong Catholic and a traditional Indian as well. I wondered then, how come these priests need to be abusive, even to him? One Priest used to make horns on his head, towards my Dad.

"Thomas, you shouldn't belong to that Horn Society. Do you know who else has horns? Look at these horns, Thomas... ha, ha!" he said swaying back and forth, his hands on either side of his forehead, index fingers pointing up, with a mocking grin.

That really confused me. I used to think to myself, holy, this Priest, why does he need to act like this? If I had been older then, I would have understood this is wrong, but I just felt it then. I knew these things weren't right. My Father was very active in the community — he even helped fundraise to build a new church out in Cluny. It's still there; he really helped, along with these other men, to have a new church.

There were other people who were important in my life.

Alex Scalp Lock, he was quite a character. He lived with us quite a bit because his parents separated and my Father took him in because he was the same age and friends with my oldest brother Paul. He stayed with us, they pow-wowed, they sang together. He kept him under his wing and I used to think Alex was my brother. Alex was a nephew of my Dad. They were so close right up until my Dad died.

Alex lived at Siksika until he left for Calgary. He had a drinking problem, but he sobered up. He was a strong member of Alcoholics Anonymous. Alex was a great pow wow dancer, a world class Prairie Chicken dancer. His occupation was security, and he worked at the Stampede Corral and then at the Glenbow Museum in Calgary. He was very instrumental in Calgary at Plains Indian Cultural Survival School, and also at the Calgary Indian Friendship Centre, anything to do with helping out people. He died Sept. 13, 1988.

The other one I grew up with was Robert Sun Walk, my cousin, who passed away a few years ago. We did things together, got into mischief together. He always looked after me, even though he was a few years younger than me. He always protected me as his sister. Over the years he was very instrumental here at Siksika. He was a pow wow singer and a member of the Eagle Society. He started up this whole Blackfoot language initiative here on the Nation, where he and others would go into the schools to teach the children the Blackfoot language. He was well known, not just here in Siksika, but in Saskatchewan and down in the States. He travelled a lot. He was an outgoing, intelligent man, a very educated man. He got sick, and passed away. Even the other day this young woman at the Head Start graduation said she remembered Robert. It was really good to hear it. Robert contributed so much to culture and language here at Siksika. Even today they still talk about him.

Another person is Robert Calf. Robert was an important person in my life journey. We shared a lot, our sobriety, our healing. I call him my brother. He is the only one left of my age from my Father's side. He is now Director of a Treatment Centre for Youth on the Blood Reserve.

Unfortunately there was so much tragedy in my family. My sister

Rosemary died at the residential school from a broken neck – at about age 10. I never met her. I don't know how she died, because back in those days my parents didn't speak English, so they couldn't find out. That was the only information given to them. I should have been around to ask some questions.

Then my brother Lawrence died when he was about 16 years old of a heart condition. My oldest brother Paul died from drinking Shellac. Donald died not that long ago, then Albert. My sister Lucy was murdered here in Siksika in 1970. My Mother had 2 or 3 babies that died – from what, I don't know.

The winter of 1982 was very cold. My Father was ill in hospital in Bassano. I was worried he was dying. One evening I came out from Calgary to visit and he said Glenter, my brother of forty, had just been to visit. My Dad said, "My girl, your brother was here, he was happy. I think he was drinking." I left and went and looked for him in the bar in Bassano, then back to the bar in Cluny. There was no sign of him. The next day back in Calgary I got a call. Glenter was found with a relative, frozen to death outside his house in Cluny. About a month later my dad passed away.

Now, just my sister Marie and I are alive.

We had so much tragedy in our lives. There must have been abuse for them in the residential school where they all went, especially from the priests and nuns...there were some stories from my brothers. Of the thirty five children I started Residential School with in Grade One in 1950, only five are alive today. Most of these people died from alcohol, victims of this disease. They resorted to alcohol to cover the pain of their experience. It took them in the form of illness, accidents, suicide, or violence. All of those things say a lot.

I had to do a lot of healing to survive. I have to be thankful that I'm only one of two survivors among all my siblings. If I didn't find my purpose and work on my healing, I could have died too.

Sometimes I go back to when I was a child. Our little house had a stove in the living room. In the wintertime, we would bring coal back from the mines in the wagon. It was a long way. We would start a fire with kindling, and then get a couple of big chunks of coal burning. We would set up a bed on the floor in front of the stove. My Dad and some others would tell old stories to us. Then the old people would feel so happy they would start to sing. It was beautiful. We children laid there in the warmth together, outside was the dark and cold, the fire crackling and the Elders singing their songs. It was like a lullaby. Slowly we would drift off. We fell asleep to the old songs, and the familiar voices.

## The Indian Residential Schools

In the late 1800's, the Canadian government developed a policy involving church-run, government-funded industrial and residential schools. The purpose of the policy was to assimilate Aboriginal people into Canadian society. Attendance at the schools was mandatory.

Over time, there were a total of about 130 schools in most of the territories and provinces. The last school closed in 1996. About 150,000 Aboriginal, Inuit and Métis children were removed from their communities and forced to attend residential schools.

Within the schools, students were discouraged from speaking their language or practicing their culture. Severe punishment could result.

Students lived in poor conditions and endured physical and emotional abuse. There are also many cases of sexual abuse. Because of the institutional placement, the children had little opportunities to experience normal family life, including parenting. The attempted assimilation resulted in personal and cultural devastation for many. The effect echoed through generations.

In 1990, Phil Fontaine, of the Association of Manitoba Chiefs, called for the churches involved to acknowledge the physical, emotional, and sexual abuse endured by students at the schools.

In 2007, the federal government announced a $1.9-billion compensation package for former students. Individuals could receive payment for the common experience of having been a former student. Individuals could then make a further claim based on their substantiated abuse. The settlement also included a Truth and Reconciliation Commission to examine the legacy of the residential schools.

In June of 2008, Canadian Prime Minister Stephen Harper delivered an official apology to residential school students in Parliament. On April 29, 2009, Pope Benedict XVI expressed his "sorrow" to a delegation from Canada's Assembly of First Nations for the abuse and "deplorable" treatment that aboriginal students suffered at Roman Catholic Church-run residential schools.

Other churches implicated in the abuse apologized in the 1990's. In 2014, the Catholic Bishops of Alberta and the Northwest Territories apologized to victims of physical and sexual abuse in the schools, the separation of children from their families, and the suppression of their culture and language.

Chapter 2 **bitter olives**

I went into the residential school in September of 1950 when I was six years old. I was there for fourteen years, leaving in 1964.

Before I went into the school, I had never heard about it. All I knew was that I was going to go to school, just like my siblings went there. They never talked about what it was like. My Father said he went to residential school in South Camp on Siksika. He said the school he attended didn't have anything to do with academics. It was mainly to learn farming and how to look after cattle and horses.

When I went into the school I didn't know my English name. All I knew was my Blackfoot name that I had known since I was born. This name was in the Blackfoot language. Then they began using the name I was registered with, Ruth Scalp Lock. Even the other students would laugh if I tried to speak English. I was very confused for the longest time. I wasn't allowed to speak my language. If you didn't speak Blackfoot all week, you got a gold star on Friday. I lived in fear all those 14 years. It was really hard for me.

I went through a lot of bullying from the students and from the girls at that time. When I think back in my healing, I recognized why I was bullied. Being Cree and Blackfoot, they used to laugh at me. I guess this was because of the historical rivalry between the Blackfoot and the Cree. My Cree Grandfather used to come and get me in the wagon with the horses. He used to sit right in that wagon box and they used to make fun of him. "Look at that ugly man," they laughed, "Ruth, he's a dirty, sweaty Cree. We know he's your

Grandfather." It was so hurtful.

I was so ashamed of my Grandfather. I didn't want him to come to the school. Today I regret that I was ashamed of my Grandfather. I wish I could see him now, and tell him how badly I feel about feeling ashamed of him. I still struggle with it. I wish I had been receptive or tried to learn where my Grandfather was coming from, try to get him to teach me about the Cree language. Those things I have to sort out.

Most days at school we had to get up at seven in the morning and we prayed as soon as we got up. We had to go to Church early in the morning, then go for breakfast, pray before breakfast, and then go to the classroom for 9 o'clock, where we prayed again. Then we prayed before lunch – right in the classroom. Then we'd go down to the dining room, we prayed again. You prayed again after lunch and then at 3:30 you had to pray again. Then supper time you had to pray again – then had to do our work. Then we were in bed at seven. I missed being outside at that time – especially in spring or summer – it would be so beautiful to go for a nice walk and enjoy life.

We had a lot of duties we had to do, like cleaning everything. The Nuns would stand there watching to see how we did our work and you always had to do a good job – if not they would plow you over the head. I always remember these things, they called them clappers. They're two wooden pieces and sometimes they would hit you over the head or pull your hair. You had to be serious, you had to do your work. The Order who ran the school were French. They called us savages. Things were either "Bon" or "Sauvage". They always spoke in their language. They would slap you. I would see so many of the young women that were beat up.

We wore a dress that went below the knee. We had brown stockings on and then you had a petticoat under your dress and there was a pocket inside. They gave you three pieces of toilet paper to blow your nose and other things. They cut our hair. But if you had somebody to braid your hair, it was okay to have long hair – but most of us had short hair. It was a big change for me, because before school I was a real tomboy, out playing with the boys, riding horses. I had long braids, a shirt, jeans, and moccasins. I was quite a sight.

They had big dorms for the junior girls and boys, and then another dorm for the intermediate and the older girls, about 15-19. The boys were in a separate part of the building. You can still see the Father's house where the school was. There's a Parish Hall and a Church as well now. They took the Main dorm building out, but there is one part of the school still there. It's a big white building where they had the classrooms.

My house, the home where I was raised, was only a mile away. So I could see it, and there were many times I wanted to go home, run away and be back with my family. But I knew the Police, or the Indian Agent would come and get me, maybe put my parents in jail. People were so afraid of the authorities back then. It was lonely, especially in the evening, when it was getting dark. The evenings were the loneliest. It made me feel so scared.

It was a strange experience for me being forced into this Catholic experience. We were baptized, confirmed, first communion, and confession. All the praying, I have to admit a lot of time I was just mumbling the words, just memorized words, no feeling. And confession, what did I, a child, have to confess? So I made up sins to confess. There were so many do's and don'ts. Don't talk to boys, don't eat meat on Fridays. Everything was a sin. This seemed like a mean God, who put fear in us all of the time. It just seemed to knock the spirit out of me. This feeling of not being good, I think, made us to never feel good about ourselves. We dealt with this through alcohol later in our lives, a lot of self-destruction. It was different than the traditional spirituality we had been brought up with, our own tradition, somewhere where we belonged- the drum, the dance, the songs, our land, our history, and the comfort that came with it.

We went home at Christmas and Easter.

In the Summer, my Father used to go camping across the Bow River with our whole family and some relatives. That's when he cut hay. He sold the hay and that's how he made the Stampede money. Once they got the pay, most of Siksika would go on the train to Calgary to go to the Stampede. Stampede started on a Monday and went through to Saturday back then. We went every summer throughout my whole childhood. I was so happy being with my family, my parents, and my relatives. I had relatives on my Dad's side who always had a tipi at the Stampede.

Calgary wasn't a big city then. Where 50th avenue and MacLeod Trail is, this, to my knowledge was the edge of town, and 16th avenue to the north. Forest Lawn wasn't even part of Calgary. We camped right in the Indian Village for a few days with my Dad's cousin and her husband – Betsy and James One Gun. In the Blackfoot way, they were like my Grandparents. They had a campsite, One Gun and his wife, where the Calgary Stampede Corral is, where the Indian Village used to be. We stayed in their tipi.

One Gun was a very well known Blackfoot Elder. He was a powerful Medicine Man. He participated in all the ceremonies and I always looked up to him and his wife. As a child I used to go visit them at their house and they were quite sick. I used to go over, just across the road from our house, and cook a meal for them – fry bread, meat and potatoes, and I did their laundry by hand.

One Gun would look at me with a sad, pitiful face, one big tear on his cheek, and say to me, "One day my girl, you're going to have a real good life – you've been so good to me. I see in the future that you will do something with your life."

I always believed what One Gun said to me.

Sometimes we had a tent and camped down in Manchester, around

50<sup>th</sup> avenue. That is where some of the Siksika had their tents. There was a street car that we used to take. I remember that one time I jumped into that trolley – I was digging around in my pocket and I had five pennies – and this white guy told me it costs more than that. These people paid my fare. I always remember that because I was so afraid I would get caught without enough fare.

Later we stayed at another place, over by where the Zoo is now, by Nose Creek. I never had chocolate milk in my life. The milkman came around early in the morning where we camped. He would come with fresh milk – glass jars with chocolate milk. That was so good. That was a real treat for me. In our tent, my mother slept at one end, my Father by the door. The milkman would stick his head in and they would both talk to him. He would then answer back, "Whoever is in there talking to me has two heads!" That still makes me laugh. I always see the humor in things. Maybe it keeps me sane.

There were lots of people from all over the world at the Stampede. They used to come around and take pictures. There was no drinking at the Village. It was so nice, so good when there was no drinking.

After Stampede we would go to the Sundance on the Blood Reserve. My Father had relatives there. We would go in a wagon with horses for 2 or 3 days and we would camp. It was so good. We would also go to Hobbema, where my mother had relatives and visit there. When you speak a Native tongue – those things stayed with me. I never lost the foundation of who I was, being Blackfoot.

After Summer, we would return to the Residential School.

I never really had a boyfriend when I was at the Residential School. I was always told by my mother not to go out with boys. Some of the girls would go out on dates. I was always sheltered from that part. These girls would run away – I always wanted to run away with them. They would run away to Calgary and the police would bring them back. They would talk about going out with boys and drinking. I always listened to my mother. I was too scared to go against what she was teaching me. When I left at age 20, to me I was still a kid – I was still playing. I was still playing with paper dolls when I was 19.

I've always been on the heavy side. In the Wintertime, you had to go to another building, so sometimes we would have our coat on. One time this Nun told me, "Take your jacket off! I don't want you to melt in this classroom and leave a big grease stain on the floor." There were times I felt like kicking them. It wasn't a good experience. It was like jail. I was so confused by my experience in the residential school. It was really tough for me. I couldn't express myself. It took me a long time to speak English. I would say I went through hell all those years.

Maybe there were a few positives – I learned how to work – but I learned that at home too. I learned to be clean, and be responsible. I learned how to cook and I learned how to sew. Those are some of the good things that I keep with me. But I always tried to stay away from the Nuns or the Priests.

There was a dining room for boys on one side and girls on the other. Later on they built a dining room just for the girls. When we got older we had our own dining room for the senior girls. That was really something. We didn't have to have people looking at us and be prim and proper all the time.

One time I was working in the kitchen and there was this machine – the potato would go around and be peeled. The Nun looking after the potatoes we called the "detective," because she watched what we were doing and would tell our supervisor. You couldn't even laugh, nothing. We were in grade ten or so, and there were about four or five of us. We were cleaning the kitchen, the big pots and pans, and had to make sure everything was clean after supper one evening. Sometimes we were still hungry. We didn't know "the detective" was still in the other room. We were digging into the fridge and the pantry– there were some apples and some other good stuff. They always hid the good stuff.

We were stuffing these apples into our sleeves and other places. We were telling each other – make sure you put them in your sleeves – because we didn't want to get caught. We were stealing. We looked like Dolly Parton! We were going to share with the other girls at the dorm. Sister walked out – she was so good at peeking around the corners, the detective. She caught us and told on us. We were sent to the Principal's office and got a real good licking.

Another time I was asked to clean Father's dining room. The priest's dining room was so nice – nice table cloth, all these fancy dishes, and they had the best food in town. A couple of us girls took turns cleaning the dining room. I saw these small serving bowls full of black grapes. I put them in my pocket. When we went back to school at 1 o'clock I could feel that they were wet. I took a couple out and put them in my mouth –I started choking. They were olives, bitter black olives. Thinking I had sweet grapes, it was a nasty surprise. The nun caught me and did I ever get it!

Sister shrieked, "Ruth Mary, what are you doing? Stealing! Stealing from the Church!" How could you do this!?"

She was pounding me on the back. I wanted to cry and laugh at the same time. Even today, if I ever see black olives, I just laugh and remember that.

There was a lot of loneliness, pain, and abuse in the Residential School. I am thankful that I had a few close friends for many years at the residential school. Two of them were Theresa Big Snake Bear Chief, and another was Lilly Wolf Collar Healy.

My sister Rosemary was such a beautiful young girl of ten when she died there.

When they were children at the school, one of Rosemary's friends said to the nun, "Where is my friend, Rosemary?" Then the Nun said, "Oh, she's gone home." Her friend said," I didn't know she was going home." And the nun said, "Oh, she's gone home to Heaven."

It's been so long now. It's hard to let go even now. She would be in her mid-80's today. Just last Fall, a woman told me she saw a little girl by where the school was, walking around in a white dress, like a communion dress. I know that is how she was laid to rest. That makes me feel better. I feel her spirit here. She was an angel. She is an angel...looking over us.

Now, I'm not a Catholic, although I was baptized and confirmed. Today I don't practice the Catholic religion. I did for a while, but I never had a feeling in here, in my heart, when I went to Church. I used to think these Nuns and Priests were so miserable and so abusive. How could they be treating us like this – and yet we go to Church?

In my mind, in my heart, I always felt it wasn't right how we were treated. So, no, I was never a Catholic. I just drifted away.

Interlude- Jim Pritchard

# A Day on the Road with Ruth

It was a bright Fall day. I came to Siksika to see Ruth and visit some of the places that she talked about in her story.

I picked her up at her office and we headed out to find the effigies on the hill overlooking Cluny. We decided to call on a white neighbor whose land the hill seemed to belong to. We entered the drive. There appeared to be no one in the house, so Ruth suggested I drive into the farm yard and that I get out and go into the workshop and see if anyone was there. "One thing I am afraid of is dogs," she shared. I shared back, "Well I'm not going in, because one thing I am afraid of is a farmer taken by surprise in his workshop."

So we agreed that we would go back to the house. "You go knock on the door and if someone comes out, I will come in," was her plan, plain and simple.

So off I went and knocked on the door. First one, then two young boys happily appeared, followed by their mother, a smiling and welcoming woman. I explained that my friend, Ruth, would like to ask her some directions, and as I turned, sure enough, here comes Ruth. Quickly and easily Ruth engaged the young mother in a conversation, asking her name, and then telling her that her Father was Tom Scalp Lock, and that he knew the woman's Father.

The effigies, the woman explained, were on the next hill, but she wasn't sure where. We thanked the young mother, headed up the highway, and down the road on the next ridge. As we headed down the dirt road, we guessed where the ancient effigies were, but it was just a guess, and nothing showed up. So we decided to turn around. As we headed back up the road a truck pulled out of a farm and headed back to the highway.

"Hurry up, catch up with him and we will see if he knows," advised Ruth, "Pick it up, flash your lights at him!"

"Uh, not really comfortable with that, let's just see if I can catch up with him at the stop sign," I responded.

By the time I almost caught up he had headed down the highway. "Let's see if we can catch him," Ruth encouraged, "And flash your lights."

"He's going to think we have an emergency or something, don't want to panic him," I said.

"Well, he's getting away...oh well, maybe he will head into Gleichen and we can catch him there...well, it doesn't look like it, looks like he's going on down the highway" were Ruth's latest offerings.

"Ok well, in a few days I will go back to the woman's house and see what else I can find out. We'll find it next time, I know it," Ruth assured me.

So now I was getting it. Ruth is persistent, clear, and would not give up easily. I guess I always knew that.

After that, we stopped at the site of the former Residential School. Ruth showed me the Church her Father helped build. Then we walked around. I detected a certain wariness in Ruth, a subtle cautiousness. It was like she was totally familiar with the place, yet quiet, almost like something bad might be lurking. She spoke of some of the things that happened here. She sadly told me of the death of her sister, Rosemary here, many years ago as a young child, still so missed.

As we drove away, Ruth talked about her spiritual relationship with Christianity.

"I don't have a relationship with Christianity, as a religion."

"But I do believe Jesus is the Creator, that's the way I interpret Jesus. It's the same thing. I believe in that higher power. My higher power could be the Holy Spirit, or Jesus. In my language it means, "The one who gave me life, who created me." Holy Spirit and Jesus are the same thing. We have different terms for the Creator, but it's "the one who gave me life."

"But I don't have a relationship with Christianity. I don't go to church. I'm not a Christian, but I believe in Jesus, because where would I be today if I didn't have the Holy Spirit in my heart? I wouldn't have contentment. I wouldn't have serenity. I wouldn't be sober. "

"When I first started my healing, I went to a traditional Medicine Man. The medicine man really helped me to heal. I had arthritis years ago, and I couldn't even walk anymore. I went to the sweat lodge out at Eden Valley. They helped me so much. I was able to walk again. There's times I would talk to another Medicine Man. I feel so much like I have these gifts within myself, that I can heal myself. That's why I don't run to the medicine cabinet for an Aspirin or Tylenol. "

Then we headed south across the prairie to search for the Majorville Medicine Wheel. It had been many years since Ruth was out there, so we watched for signs, eventually turning east, heading into the hills. Passing through Majorville, literally a corner with a couple of old buildings, we drove on, winding through the blonde Autumn hills.

At one point we entered a series of turns, marked by a sign, "Winding Road." It sure was. Ruth added it was a good symbol of her life, the ups and downs and many strange turns. She pointed out a straight line of electrical poles that ran alongside the snaking road, "That's my life, a line I see running straight that guides me through all the challenges, at times when I was almost lost."

Today we seemed to be lost. Eventually coming to a ranch, we drove up to the house, again no sign of anyone. We decided to proceed into the yard, and repeated the earlier interaction. Ruth: one thing I am afraid of, dogs. Jim: I don't walk into farmer's workshops unannounced, sorry. So that was that, no sign of anyone, so we started out again. Then we saw a man come onto the drive behind us, preceded by a dog. Ruth stayed in the car.

He was friendly enough. I asked him the whereabouts of the Medicine Wheel. He said, keep heading east until the road comes to a T, then turn south and keep following it until you come to the highline, then turn, keep going until you cross a cattle gate, then turn and keep going….Ok, thanks very much, have a good day. We were basically following our nose.

We found our way to the highline, and a T in the road. Which way did he say to turn? West, I think. Off we went, up a hill, then to a point where the road turned to a grass trail, and off in the distance a row of humpy hills stretched across the horizon. That would be the place, I guessed. But we weren't sure, and thought, let's head back to the T and try east and see if there was anything more obvious. So off we went, up another hill, until we came to a cattle guard, where we stopped, and mutually agreed, neither of us really knows where we are going, so maybe this isn't the day. Maybe this is just the day to explore.

We headed back the way we came, until Ruth said, "Stop here, we need to look at this rock. I know it is powerful." There was a large stone beside the road, with obvious markings on it. Ruth stepped out onto the brown grasses, the sun bright, and the wind rising, reflecting on the moment.

"I feel very good to be here today, close to the Medicine Wheel. It is important to stop here by this stone. Stones are important to our people, for healing, for marking, for identity. To find the Wheel, I should have made an offering this morning, but I was too busy. Today is not the day."

"To be here, I think back to when my ancestors roamed this area. I can feel them here, on my back I feel it, my Blackfoot ancestors, even some of my nomadic Cree ancestors. On this rock I see the markings of what has passed. This is how teachings are passed. I learned this from my Dad, my Grandparents, and my ancestors."

"This is a beautiful day, the sunshine, the land. It is close to Fall, another season coming. It is time to enjoy what the Creator gave us today. I feel good, at home on this sacred land. No cost can be attached to it."

"We have to take the time to appreciate the beauty around us. Once I walked like a zombie. I had no eyes to see, no ears to hear. Look at the beauty around us, the sun, the water there, sacred, even the wind, how it blows more as the day goes on."

"Even though we didn't find what we came for, it hasn't been a wasted day. We need to stop and acknowledge everything around us...this rock, being here, it will always be."

We didn't find the Medicine Wheel that day, but we found other things. It was a good day.

# Part II

# Falling

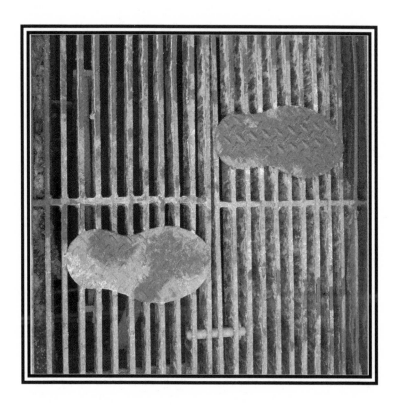

"One fork, one spoon. I was alone. I had nothing."

## Chapter 3 wake up now...you must decide

I graduated from the residential school in June of 1964. I was so happy to come out. I had this feeling of freedom.

The Father we had at the time got us work at the Provincial Training School in Red Deer. The Training School placement was supposed to be to learn to take care of people with mental handicaps, a kind of a nursing course. We were interacting with patients, doing shift work. I worked in the kitchen and dining room a lot of the time.

We didn't have school counseling about career choices where we could go. I was hoping to further my education, and I think if I had career counseling I would have made some better choices for myself. It was kind of forced on me by this other person.

We stayed in the Nurses Residence. I was very lonely being so far away from home for the first time. I just couldn't get used to being away, because it was like culture shock...away from home, away from family. I was away for two years.

That's when I started to drink. The first time I really got drunk I blacked out. This lady helped me up the stairs to my room. I was crawling. I woke up the next morning. I didn't know where I was. Little did I know I had fallen into a life of drinking that would last ten years, like wandering in the wilderness.

I knew I had a problem and I couldn't handle alcohol, but it just progressed. Alcohol filled a need, it made me feel happy, covered up the years of pain and abuse- serious abuse - the put downs, the emotional and verbal abuse, bullying among my peers, physical and sexual abuse. So much. I was confused when I left the residential school, confusion between the spiritual parts of the Catholic Church and my traditional beliefs. Who was I? What was my path? I was a traditional person taught to fear an angry, mean God who said I was never good enough. We were sinners and we would go to Hell...I didn't know.  One thing I know now is that I was a traumatized person, with a deep rooted hurt.

Drinking gave me confidence for a while, helped me express myself, and I didn't have to deal with my problems. It was like a magic potion, made me feel better, and the memories would be faded. But it just got worse. I just got more sick. I didn't have a focus in life, never had a purpose in my heart. I was just going with the flow.

I moved to Calgary and met up with this lady, Mary, and I stayed with her. She had a family, a husband and children. She was a Native woman, pretty with dark hair. I must have met her through drinking at the bar. They were drinkers too. I would babysit for her when they went out. That man, he was quite an abuser. He used to always beat her up and I'd run out with the kids and her.  I had been aware of domestic violence before, but this was the first time I had seen this off the reserve. I didn't think white men beat their wives, and all the drinking and swearing. I was surprised to see this.

We lived on the main floor of a house. Upstairs was rented out, like a rooming house for men. There was always something going on, partying and fighting, and downstairs too with Mary and her husband and kids. I remember one time, when Mary had to run out of the house half dressed. The next day she was covered in bruises.

I got into a secretarial course at the Modern College of Business. I wanted to go there.  I was kind of looking around for something to do, so I went to Indian Affairs and asked them if I could take a course and they paid for the tuition. They gave me a living allowance and I stayed at that woman's house. It wasn't a very pleasant place to live, but I didn't have far to go to school. I took typing, shorthand, filing and office duties.

After school, I would go get drunk, go to the Queen's Hotel, the Imperial Hotel. Sometimes I would go with Mary, or other friends that I met.

I was drinking to cover the pain. It wasn't a social thing. You know how some people have a drink or go to a party one night, then the next day they'd go on with life again. It wasn't that way.

I couldn't get up early. I went to the bar on Wednesday night, Thursday night. Sometimes I didn't go home at night. I'd go out to the bar at five after school. I just stayed out, and maybe run into someone, and then go party with them. I didn't really have good friends. I'd find friends, and I'd go party with them, pass out. The next morning, if I was lucky enough to get up in time, I would go to school. It was such a merry-go-round. I'd go find a place to shower. There were times I would quit drinking maybe a week or so, but not long enough to really look at the problem. Eventually I quit going to the Business College.

I lasted about five months. I didn't even get a certificate from there. I was booted out by the Supervisor there, "Ms. Scalp Lock, I need to talk with you. When you started we thought you were committed to learning and getting ahead. But now it appears you are not. You are not showing up, or coming in late, not how you work in the business world. I am sorry, but you will be discharged from the Program. Good luck."

I didn't care. Didn't matter. That was my attitude at the time.

Then I had my children, Karleen and Trevor, about two years apart. We moved to Regina. There was really a lot of problems, more of the alcohol and all that goes with it, what my life had become. I worked as a file clerk typist at Indian Affairs in Regina. The children spent quite a bit of time with their Grandmother, in Saskatchewan.

Eventually I left. I came back to Calgary. I started to drink again.

Just recently, I was driving down the street in Forest Lawn in Calgary with my husband now, Francis Melting Tallow. We were behind this yellow cab and I could see the passenger in the back. He kept opening the door. He was trying to jump out. Oh my gosh, this guy, I can relate to him. He jumped out of the cab and he started running. These are reminders, because I did that so many times when I was drinking! I'd get into a taxi cab and I'd give them a phony address, and I knew in the back of my mind I didn't have any money and that eventually I would jump out of the cab.

There was a lot of wild stuff going on that summer in 1973.

One time I was in a taxi cab and there were other women in that cab with me. Me, of course, I was a leader, some phony leader. I guess I always wanted to impress my drinking buddies. Most of them are not here today. They died from alcohol. The cab driver told us about the fare, and asked to see it, so I was digging in my purse. He knew we didn't have it so he just started pounding on my head, trying to grab my purse away from me. I never got my purse back! He was driving us to the police station. We all jumped out of the cab, and I was just thinking about myself. I didn't care about the women sitting in the back. I jumped out just before we got to the police station and I started running. I was so scared and I was kind of sobering up. I didn't know what to do. I ran into the old Calgarian Hotel, ran out the back door, went in to the Regis Hotel and was kind of looking around to see if I knew anybody to buy me a drink. I couldn't see anybody. I ran out the backdoor again. So I saw another cab parked on the west side of the York Hotel. I got in and, of course I sat in the back and I managed to jump out of the cab before we got to my house. He didn't do anything. He just had to take it. I was really great for doing those things. I didn't care when I was drinking.

I worked at the Calgary Indian Friendship Centre. I was sober for a little while, maybe a year. I was working as a receptionist, and I had my own place.  Then I started to drink again, and ended up in Winnipeg, Manitoba. These years were a fog, there was no clarity.

When I was in Winnipeg, there were times I went and slept in what they called the Main Street Project. That's where all the homeless drunks would go. I would go sleep there.  I would bum around for a drink, go into a hotel trying to find somebody to buy me a drink.

When you have this alcohol addiction, it doesn't matter what you do to get a drink. You live to drink. I went from one job to another, just waiting for pay day. I stole vanilla from the corner store. The police knew me by my first name. I hated Sundays, because that's when I tried to sober up, but sick from the alcohol. The only cure was to start over.

I was pretty violent when I was drinking. I don't know how many fights I got into, beat up on people. There were times I was thrown in jail, for creating a disturbance, but nothing like a major charge. I was often the leader, me and "my partners in crime," looking for some easy mark to get drunk and take their money. Now I ask for forgiveness for anyone I hurt.

Sometimes I'd wake up in the drunk tank. Once I was beat up and ended up in the General Hospital in Calgary. Another time, in a black out, me and a friend woke up in Edmonton, how I don't know, and started to walk back, ending up hitch hiking. I hate to say it, but sometimes I would throw up and I would wake up, my face would be right in it.

---

March 14, 1974. That night, my friend and I drank up our rent and our damage deposit money. We were supposed to pay on a place. We were just drinking around the town that night. We was sitting in this all night restaurant, and this white guy was just laughing at me. I must have looked really funny.

In a crazy daze, thinking to myself, why are you looking at me? Laughing at me? I know that look, it makes me feel terrible. I just needed to stop it, how it made me feel.

I went over to him and I pulled his hair and threw him on the floor. They called the cops. I ran out and my friend came running after me. I was drunk. I came to when I was running down the street. My friend said, "Gee, that guy...you went and threw him off the stool and you were going to beat him up. "

The first hotel we went in that night was the Winnipeg Inn, the big shot hotel. I don't know how in the world they gave us a room. My friend must have paid for it. We went into the room, and I was so sick. Just when I started to sober up, I wanted to drink again. There was a liquor cabinet. I busted it open. My friend was passed out and I started to drink. It was now the dark heart of the night.

I was just sitting there, feeling helpless and hopeless. I had to do something about my life. I passed out. Then I'd sit up and drink again. It was like I was fighting it, this voice that was trying to talk to me.

Then I had this spiritual awakening. I heard a voice out of nowhere. I have heard this a few times in my life at important times. It was a calm and caring voice. The voice spoke to me in a deep and clear voice, "Ruth, it is time to wake up. Find your strength again... find a path, and help yourself... and your people... I am here to help you... Wake up now... You must decide. "

Then I talked to myself, "What is happening? Am I dying? ...What have I become?... a daze of alcohol and pain...I am lost... I am in pain...Lost in confusion and darkness...What has happened to me and my people?"

I really felt something in my heart. I just started to cry. Somebody was telling me, Ruth, you have got to do something. I was just sitting there crying. I could have stayed all night and the next day and drank all that liquor.  I could have kept on with this, until my life ended early...

I got up and walked to the bathroom, and poured all the liquor down the toilet. Then I walked back into the room.

I told my friend, "I'm going to phone the hospital. I don't know if you want to come with me... I'm done with drinking. "

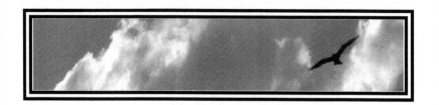

Chapter **4** the loneliest day in my life

We left the room, called a taxi, and went to the hospital.

They had a detox center to "dry out" alcoholics. I just sat there.

I started to pray. That was the first time I ever prayed. I wanted to get some help and to follow through. I kept crying. I couldn't even drink water.

Then a lady came, and they were asking me where I wanted to go for treatment. They gave me a paper with names of places. I told them I'd like to go to a place that's out of town. I didn't want to be in a downtown area in a treatment centre. There were two counsellors. One was a Native woman, Virginia.

I told Virginia, "I'm just tired of myself... just hate myself... I want to do something about my life.... I'm done."

They took me out to a Program called X-Kalay. It is now called the Behavioural Health Foundation. It reminded me of the old Father Lacombe Center in Midnapore, in Calgary. It was previously run by the Oblate Fathers a long time ago. That was in St. Norbert, Manitoba, part of Winnipeg. The Church gave it to this treatment centre that was started in Vancouver. X-Kalay is interpreted from Cree and means "the unknown path." That makes sense to me because I was lost and didn't know what path I was on. It was new to me. I didn't know where it would go. It was the loneliest day of my life.

I had arrived at the hospital mid-morning. I got out to St. Norbert in the early evening. There was a sign at the door, "Today is the first day of the rest of your life." I didn't know what that meant then. But now I will never forget it.

Eventually I fell asleep for a long time. I didn't wake up until early evening the next day. I woke up like in a dream. I didn't know where I was, and who these strange people were. I felt like running away. I thought I had made the wrong decision to come here. But where would I go? I had no money to go anywhere.

The withdrawal from alcohol took a few days. Then the hard part started. It was so hard to do, make this huge change and break from what I knew. I was sick, so sick. I had to take medicine to calm my nerves.

The treatment process brought out a lot of pain. I just wanted to hide from it. I was afraid of all the memories of abuse in the residential school, flashbacks of the crazy things I did when I was drunk. The whole process of treatment brought fear. I couldn't look anyone in the face. I tried to lie my way through everything. I could have left. But where would I be now?

I was so lonely, terribly lonely. I missed my friends, because even though we were drinking, they were my friends, and we had fun, some good times. And I missed my children so badly. They were with their Father and his Mother. It was tough. Oh, I never want my grandchildren to see me like I was. It breaks my heart to think of it.

I wanted to leave, to run away, back to my life and my friends, the things I knew. At times I wished I had never come here. Maybe it was a stupid thing to do.

For the first thirty days, I didn't call anyone. After that I began calling my sisters, my kids, and of course my Father. I always left him messages that I was OK. I stayed in touch with these important people, and I knew I was not alone.

I stayed there for three months. For me, that was the end of the drinking. They saved my life. I am sure of that to this day.

I left and went to Saskatoon. I had a job working at St Michael's hospital for a couple of months. I was sober.

This was when I really got into my spirituality. I was going to counselling, plus attending the Alcoholics Anonymous program. I was socializing with people that didn't drink or go to the bars where there's temptation. I just had to make up my mind.

I was praying to the Great Spirit. When I imagine the Great Spirit, I always see a light, a white light. The spiritual aspect was so genuine because it was coming from my heart. It was like a door that had been locked was now opened. I always prayed to find a purpose, to give me the strength.

A lot of times I talked to myself, using self- talk, "Ok Ruth, you are doing good. You are doing OK now. You are going to be alright. You never had compliments, only put downs, you wouldn't even know how to take them. So give yourself a compliment, and accept it."

I wasn't smudging, burning sweet grass, not until I came home. I didn't really get to meet Elders then. I started to work. I rented this basement suite. But oh, I was lonely, and really down and out in my living situation. How could anybody live like that? I was lucky if I had a blanket. I think I had a sheet, a pillow. It was a furnished apartment. Otherwise I would have been sleeping on the floor.

Inside, my thoughts went back and forth, "I have nothing, one fork, one plate, that's all I have. All this work and this is all I have now. Not a family, not my children. I need to be strong, listen to the Great Spirit, listen to what my Father told me... Am I strong enough? I have to keep my eye on the path, and be strong. Ruth, you made your decision, it is now or maybe never. Be strong...am I strong enough?"

I sobered up, March, April, May, June, July, August, probably about six months. Then I went and got my children, Karleen and Trevor, from their Grandmother's where they had been staying, and I came home to Calgary. We came home for the weekend, and my Father met us in Calgary at the Greyhound bus depot. We went and got a room at the Summit Hotel. I had a room there and I found out that they were looking for a secretary at a treatment center for Native people. So I went to apply. They told me right there that I had a job, to start Monday. This was around November of 1974. I was the secretary and receptionist. I did things like taking the minutes for their Board meetings.

I had a two bedroom apartment not far from the Holy Cross Hospital. I had my kids and my Father used to come and stay with us and babysit. Karleen started school.

I felt I was starting the path to my purpose, that I had found my spirituality. It all took time. I knew that I would have to contribute to society, to work, and do things like pay rent and pay income tax. I felt good about it, to be responsible for the first time in my life. That sounds funny. I went grocery shopping and I dressed up. It took a long time to start looking at myself, to look good, to get up in the morning, go to work, live life instead of just bumming around.

My job was really good. I was there for about a year. But I always felt I could help people more, to help them to heal from alcohol. So, I went to work with a recovery center. I was an intake counsellor, the only Native person working there.

It really helped me personally to see alcoholics coming into detox. There were people from all walks of life. It happened to Native people, poor people, uneducated people, there were lawyers, doctors too, you name it. Alcohol can get to a person regardless of their background. As they say, alcohol has no respect. It doesn't care who you are, or what you've done in your life.

Not all people had respect. Of course, they were not well, and going through their healing. This one guy, a lawyer, I always remember he said, "Why are you working here? Why don't you go and work where you come from? There must be lots of drunken Indians there." Holy, I was so hurt by this comment, the drunken Indian. Well, I understand this guy was in alcoholism, and now, in my healing, I can forgive. How do they know all the trauma that we have experienced that leads to the drinking?

It's like the women who does my hair now. One day she asked me, "How come you people drink so much?" I turned to her and said, "That's a good question, but not a short answer."

At the recovery center people would come in, we'd do the assessment and sometimes if they were in a really bad state, they would take them to the hospital. They'd keep them at the hospital and then they'd come back. At that time they stayed in treatment for seven days. The Twelve Step approach is something I could really relate to, seeing how alcohol interfered with my life. It took time to really understand it. The spiritual part is most important to me, believing in a higher power, believing in a power that's greater than me.

I was at the center for two years. I left there to take a Life Skills Course. After that, my coach helped me get into the Life Skills Coach Training program in Edmonton. It was for people who just wanted to learn more. It was up to them if they wanted to go further and become a life skills coach. Life Skills really did a lot of good for me, learning how to express myself and how to deal with problems. This course taught me coping skills, and how to run groups.

I did get my certificate to become a facilitator, the first I ever got, which make me proud. With Life Skills I began to understand that if I'm having problems, there are problem solving skills that I can use in my life. When you are doing a group, you can teach people to use these skills in their lives. For example, sometimes I get a gut feeling in reaction to something. Right there, I know it is a feeling and I have to identify that feeling and express it. I would say, "I feel mad, or angry when you..." You always attach a feeling with a behaviour, "I feel mad or upset when you put me down or make fun of me...." This was new for me, this being aware of myself and what was going on with others. It played a big part in my healing, getting control after all the years of abuse and drinking.

When I finished the course, I came back to Calgary. I started to do life skills training at the Native Friendship Centre with funding that I was able to obtain. Step by step, I was coming into myself, getting on my feet. I was moving ahead.

# Part III

# Learning to Walk Again

"I remembered what One Gun had said."

## Chapter 5 profession and tradition

A new opportunity opened up for me working as a Native Liaison worker with Child Welfare in downtown Calgary. That is where I met Jim Pritchard, who was a social worker there. The Social Workers would refer some of their Native clients who needed support and help. These were families whose children had been removed because of family problems, often because of problems with alcohol. My role was to connect with the families and help them get their children back, help them through the system, including the law and the courts.

I always felt it was important to me to be able to go to the case conferences and put in my "two bits worth." It recognized my professionalism, meaning the traditional part of what I'm doing with the people. The workers were supportive of me, and acknowledged the importance of having Native people to work with these families that have their children in government care.

I remember I used to go looking for the clients downtown, so that we could connect and work with them. I was able to track them down. It wasn't that hard because I knew all the places where they hung out because of my own experience a few years before! Someone had to do this, because they don't feel good to come to an office. Sometimes I would take them to a park, maybe Central Park close to our Office, have something to eat with them, and start that connection. It took a while for our people to start coming to the office.

I explained the Child Welfare system to the families, what happens when their child is removed from them, and all of the legalities, what they had to do if they had to go to court. I would take them to court and explain everything to them.

But they had to have a role to play, their responsibility. They would need to work with our services and those trying to help them. I would go to home visits, do a lot of work with them around alcohol, take them to an AA meeting or take them to Native Alcohol Services. They felt good. I used to tell them I'm not a Child Welfare person. I work like a liaison to work with them and the system. The more they worked with our services, the better things would go for them in court. I explained that you can't be working against the system if you want to get your children back. There are reasons why children are apprehended, and things that needed to change in their lives.

I had to earn their trust in me as part of the system. I ran up against that and of course it took time.

"Oh Ruth, we know you, remember when we used to drink together back on the res and downtown. We had a lot of fun together. Are you just one of them now?...you think you're better than us. You're just an apple now, eh?" I just laughed, that always works, just be a little silly.

But you have to hang in and work with people. It helped that I spoke the Blackfoot language. I explained it to them, don't take me for an apple. What I mean by apple is I'm Indian on the outside and white on the inside.

Of course it is understandable that there was a lack of trust in the system. In Calgary and back here at Siksika, they don't know how to approach the workers. They're in fear, especially the ones that experienced residential schools. There was huge fear and distrust of anything to do with authority. They like it when they know there's a

Native person to work between them and the workers, to really understand them. As long as that liaison person works intensively with the Aboriginal families and really does the work and keeps acknowledging them, "Okay, we've done this work and this is going to help you in court." But you have to build that trust, even with me I had to build that trust. That's why I went looking for them. We just had a social time and they felt much better that way.

Working with parents, I always believe that word "should" is kind of an order. In my way of interviewing people, I always ask them, "Do you think this might be a good way to do this?" I try to give them some choice, the options and something to really look at. "Should," I always feel, is an order. Maybe it's not good for this person. Try to give them choices.

I was trusted by the Child Welfare workers in Calgary, to drive all of the children to Siksika to visit with their families over the weekend. I was trusted to do this. Then I would bring them back on Monday. Sometimes I'd take a whole Saturday to take the kids to Siksika, maybe for a five hour visit. I always explained to parents that those visits had to be supervised. And those reports really helped in court. They got their kids back. It is all about building trust, and being with people. That's what I always tell people who work with these families, even now, all people who work in Child Welfare need to learn how to do this. I did this work for four years. It really gave me an understanding of how Child Welfare works, and how helpful it is to have Native people work with our families. We returned a lot of children to their families.

When I left that work I took a job working as an adult probationer officer at Siksika, on my Reserve. I supervised the probationers, overseeing their conditions and doing work with the Courts. I did home visits with probationers. If they breached their probation, I had to take them back to court. I was told, "You cannot go looking for your probationers. It's their responsibility."

There were times I had to take probationers back to court when they breached their conditions. This one Elder was just crying, "Ruth, why do you have to breach my probation?" and I explained to him, "My friend, you know you are not supposed to be drinking. Sure, I know you are home when I am here to see you, but you know the condition about drinking. I'm sorry."

It would break my heart when this happened.

So it was often a struggle within me. I wanted to be compassionate and help, but there were the orders of the Court. Of course, I understood the need for this. It was just really hard for me. I had to do a pre-sentence report based on my meetings with my clients, and then the Crown would put me up on the stand to ask questions. I had to write down exactly what the probationer said.

I left after a couple of years because it was not a good fit for me. I felt for these people and I knew in my heart these people have hope.  It was very strict, and it really bothered me. I couldn't last long on that job, only a couple of years.

At this point I was in the middle of trying to transfer back to be reinstated as a member of the Siksika Band. In my first marriage, I transferred from Siksika and became a member of his Band in Saskatchewan.  It took time to go through the divorce and I had to get a letter from the Indian agent where my ex-husband was from, which was part of Treaty 4, to let me transfer back to Siksika.  There was a lot of paperwork and meetings that had to be done. There were some people on the Council that I approached, to see if they could accept me back into Siksika.

This was before the whole political issue around Bill C 31. Bill C 31 was about a group of women who took the Canadian Government to court. This group of women organized throughout Canada to take on the Indian Act, which said Native women who married a non-Native would lose their Indian status and benefits. The person that led the whole movement was named Jean Corbiere. She was a Native woman who had married a non-native and she lost her treaty rights. These women fought for years. Finally, they won their case in the Supreme Court of Canada and with that they won their Treaty Status back. It was a long struggle.

Because of the Court decision, all the reserves in Canada had to come up with their own membership code to decide who could be a member of their Band, for those women and their children who had lost their status. I realized I could end up with a problem. I could still be out in limbo in Treaty 4. Maybe I wouldn't have been able to transfer from Treaty 4. This did not feel fair to me. If I had married within Treaty 7, I would be allowed back in. But because I married outside, I had this big problem. It didn't seem right. I was Blackfoot from birth. How could I not be a member, and have the rights and benefits of a Blackfoot person?

There was all this controversy about Band membership for some Aboriginal women. My Father knew these things I might be running up against about my Band membership. He said I needed to hurry, meet with the Chief and Council, and get accepted back into Siksika. My Father never went wrong, in all the things he told me. He prepared me in so many different ways. My Father knew my marriage never worked out, and all these things take time, the divorce, and the transfer back. If I hadn't listened to my Father, who knows where I would be today?

I was so lucky, so fortunate. I always thank the Holy Spirit for helping me get these things in place. I went to approach Chief and Council before all these things came into effect. They gave me a letter saying that I was a Siksika member and signed a Band Council Resolution, a legal document. That's how I was able to transfer back to Siksika with my children. In 1985, I became a Siksika member again. Me and my children.

I lived not far from the Crowfoot Ferry, on the east end of Siksika, by the Bow River. It was a two-bedroom house with no basement. I obtained a job in Bassano, a small town not far from Siksika. It was in the school with Golden Hills School Division, where a lot of our children were bussed to school. I had a big role in starting up a Native Program. That program is still in operation today. My pay was coming from Golden Hills and I was reporting to Siksika education. It was a partnership. I started out right at Bassano school for a year, working with the children, liaising with their families here at Siksika. I was working with the kids that were having problems with absenteeism and kids that had behaviour problems at school. My late cousin, Robert Sunwalk, used to come out, as well as other Elders. We taught the children about our Siksika way. I was teaching Blackfoot to the students. Even the non-Blackfoot students used to come in. They were interested in learning the language.

I worked with the parent advisory group. We had group meetings out in the Cluny area on a regular basis. I'd ask them what kind of problems they are having, what kind of things they would like to see changed, right down to the bus routes, any problems they had. I kept track of kids coming into school. If kids were having problems with absenteeism, they would ask me, how come this child is having so many problems coming to school? I would go out and see them and their families.

Siksika was really "gung-ho" about helping our kids get an education. They always had that mentality to really work with the kids when they went off to these white schools.

I have always felt that your attitude is so important in your work. You really have to be professional and to understand who you're working for and who you're working with. You have to make sure you work with the Principal and the teachers. You have to be open minded, always ready to hear the other side and learn. You have to use discretion, respect confidentiality, including what happens at the school. But if I see anything wrong, I would address it. I don't go out into the community and start talking about it, because there is some confidential stuff that should stay at work. You have to have those boundaries, respect what happens at work. Otherwise, it spreads like wildfire, and gets all twisted. The main thing about being a liaison is bringing people together, don't just act like a shuttle, taking information back and forth. You need to bring people together, so that they can talk to one another directly. It's not for me to speak for people, but have them speak for themselves, and for me to help them do that. Get the families talking to the school about their children.

It seems a lot of my career at that stage was as a "Native Liaison." I guess that reflects a purpose for me, to work to build bridges from the Aboriginal to the non-Aboriginal world. I spent my early life in my world, and then many years in the non-Aboriginal world. Now, I am back in my first world. But they need to be connected. So, in this role, you bring an awareness of the Native perspective. I also bring knowledge to our People, of how various programs and services work, because they can be so intimidated by all these systems. If you don't understand it, don't sign! Mostly, it is about opening communication so people can talk, learn, and begin to understand each other.

Our People have been given many labels, Indian, Native, Aboriginal, who knows what next. This is why I jump around using these terms, depending on the situation and who I am talking to. It's frustrating, like we can't identify ourselves. I do not consider myself an Aboriginal. I don't like the term. To tell you the truth, I was always proud to be an Indian, to be called an Indian. As long as you respect me for it. Like I do.

Even today I am always involved with the community surrounding Siksika. For example I recently went out and gave a talk on the Medicine Wheel. The Medicine Wheel is our way of seeing life, as a whole, meaning the physical, emotional, mental, and spiritual. It also means the directions, the seasons of the year, and the seasons of life. I like to share, empower and encourage, particularly the young. That is so important.

While I was doing the school project, I had a one year contract with the Glenbow Museum in Calgary. I worked on "The Spirit Sings" Exhibition for the 1988 Olympics. This was an exhibit to honor the

Aboriginal People of this land. This is also when I started to work at the shelter for women in Calgary. I was busy! I was still living out at Siksika, over an hour away.

Working on The Spirit Sings was just like being at home because everyday, I would see the artifacts. I have always had questions to do with certain things about myself and my culture. I even found a picture of my late Dad, as he was one of the first old-style Chicken Dancers. These dancers dress up like the prairie bird, and imitate them, the way they move, like they become the bird. I found so much information. I really enjoyed my role. I was, of course, a native liaison! They should have had a different name for my role, because mainly I was working with our People. I used to pick up the Elders at Siksika and bring them into Calgary to the Glenbow. Their role was to bring their knowledge, storytelling, how to make bannock, or how to make costumes. They all had some sort of expertise to bring to the table. When the visitors started coming from different parts of the world, these Elders were there to share their knowledge and wisdom.

I was also an interpreter, especially for the Siksika Elders that didn't speak English. We would go up on stage and I would introduce myself and the Elder. Oh, I had fun. One time, this one Elder, I introduced him and I got my numbers mixed up. He was 82 years old, but when I spoke in English I said 79 and the Elder was so offended. He said, "I'm not 79, I'm 82 years old!" Of course I started laughing! There's always some kind of humorous thing that happened to me. But my late uncle Alex Scalp Lock, he was security, was peeking around the corner. He just looked ashamed of me, because of my mistake with the number.

Alex said, "Ruth, you're getting up in age, I'm not very happy with you. You should know your numbers in our language."

I felt so bad. I felt I had let people down and that I should have known better.

I had come along way from the night I woke up in 1974. I was walking confidently. I was working with my People, learning how systems worked, and bringing white and Indian people together. I was trying to create understanding.

There was much more I could do, for myself, and to give to others. I remembered what One Gun had said. I had a purpose, things I could do with my life.

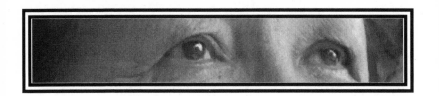

## Chapter 6 the vision and the shield

A dream came to me.

In my vision, I was shown our women, and not just women, but the whole family crying out to have a place, a shelter, where families could be healed from violence and abuse. I knew in the vision that our People cannot continue living like this. I knew it was going to take a long time to change, to make it happen. And I remember a man in the dream, an older white man, walking with me.

In this dream I felt that our people had known so much abuse in our past, by the reserve system, different statuses and rights, sexual, physical, and cultural abuse at the residential schools. Drinking to numb the pain. Violence had become part of our communities. We had to stop the abuse, the abusing patterns between ourselves that we had learned and passed on between us. We had to protect our vulnerable, and rebuild our families, and our communities. We needed to create safety to do this work. This would have to be in a way that made sense and worked for us. We needed to do it in a way built on our history and culture as a People. We had to do it together, our Elders, our leaders and our grassroots people. We had to work with others, but we needed to heal ourselves, because we were not confident in ourselves to be strong with others yet. We needed to heal.

This dream now lived in my heart, and that's where I kept it, and it continued to grow.

I began to work on this vision, while I worked on all my other jobs.

At a women's shelter in Calgary I was a crisis counsellor, a front line worker. I was the only Native worker at any of the Calgary shelters at the time, as far as I knew. I don't know why there weren't more Native workers in the shelters, because our women were being sent there and were working with them.

I always wanted to do more and to give more, so I even worked on the switchboard. Just like I didn't have enough work to do! I was also working part time at an alcohol treatment center for women in Calgary. It was in a big beautiful mansion.

Working as a crisis front line worker at the women's shelter, I worked with a team. I worked with Mary Jane Amy, June Wiggins, and many others. We were just like one big happy family. One of them cut my hair, because she was a hair stylist. One would do my files from my notes. All these counsellors were always willing to do something for me. Mary Jane was the supervisor and she was one hell of a woman too! Most of the supervisors I've known are usually very strict and everything has to be just-so, but Mary Jane was so good to work with.

I really worked well with these counsellors, and then I shared my dream with them. I was the only Native counsellor and there were four shifts. When I was not on shift, the Native women didn't have anyone to counsel them in our way. I didn't only focus on the Native women because the other clients who were not Native wanted to talk to me too, so I never focused just on the Native women. I tried to do my work with the other women who wanted counselling support. But my coworkers felt all along that we needed more Native counsellors at the shelters.

I remember once I was coming on to the night shift. One of the counsellors said, "I'm so concerned about one of the residents. I think she's doing drugs because I can smell pot coming from her room." In my heart I knew she was wrong, but I didn't say anything.

So we went down to her room, and we knocked on the door, and that lady opened the door - here she was burning sweet grass. She was working on healing herself in the traditional way. I just laughed to myself.

I was then hired full time, and I had to get more formal education, so I enrolled in the University of Calgary and took some psychology and sociology courses. They let me go to class and still get paid for it. But I found it so stressful working and I had my two kids. It was really hard for me working in Calgary while living out at Siksika, more than an hour's drive away, so I moved back to Calgary. I was back in Calgary and had all these things going. I did a lot of moving around. One of my grandchildren needed support, so I was really thinking about it, maybe we should just move back to Siksika. But I kept thinking about this dream to start a new shelter for Native women.

So many different incidents over time supported the need for a Native women's shelter, and I documented them all, including the way Indian Affairs did things with the women. I had a run-in with a manager at Indian Affairs in Calgary.

"These women come to the City for protection, they need shelter. Then what do you give them? You put them downtown in a skid row hotel. This does not help them. It only sets them up for failure. I think we can do better than to put them in a place like this. "

I knew this from my own experience on the streets. There's too much temptation. That's why in Winnipeg I chose to go out of town for treatment. Women need a safe and healthy place to recover.

It was time to start moving ahead. I organized our very first meeting. It was in Eau Claire, at Diane Melting Tallow's apartment. My late uncle Alex was there. We started talking about my vision, where I was shown the need of our people. I knew I needed support, more people to help me. I needed to find a person that could really help me from their experience in the community, getting people together and getting things going, someone who was genuine. I realized that the man walking in my dream was Nelson Gutnick. I had been shown Nelson in my dream, as a person who could help me. Nelson was a person who had been in and out of my life over the years. First, I knew him in Fort Qu'appelle in Saskatchewan, when Nelson was a Community Development Officer with Indian Affairs. Then I knew him later in Calgary when he was a social worker with Indian Affairs and he helped me. He tried to get me out of the gutter back then. Now Nelson was with the Social Work Department at the University of Calgary. So I called Nelson who talked with me and he came on board. Alex, Diane, Nelson, and then others, would come to these meetings which became our working committee. I knew I needed alot of help, I told people I needed to rack their brains, I needed their guidance and expertise. Some of the people got so frustrated. It is long hard work, starting from nothing. A dream is one thing, but it takes hard work.

Nelson was saying we have to have statistics, numbers, you can't just go to the government and give them a "big sob story." You have to go into the Native community, and you have to have support from the leadership in Treaty Seven. You need the community behind you to support the work.

We were able to get some funding to get a needs assessment done. We went into the Native community, and to the Indian Friendship Center. We invited so many people to come and talk with us and to be a part of this development.

Alderman Bob Hawkesworth, Barb Scott and Mayor Al Duerr really supported us. We would meet with the Mayor and Council of Calgary. They had a big Native committee. We went to all these people to get them involved and supporting us.

There were so many meetings, on and on. There were times I felt like giving up. I would really pray hard. I would phone Nelson, who had become my right hand man. Nelson's approach was to support me, my vision to have a traditional shelter, but then to ask, you have a goal, now what are you going to do? His approach worked for me.

One night, I was lying in bed, and I was really thinking about my next move. I was working on the needs assessment, and lots of stuff was happening. I was crying that night. Then another vision came to me. I was shown what to do and not to give up, that it was going to get easier. I could really see these people, Holy People, helping me, just like they were holding my hand to continue. Spirit was telling me, you can't quit in the middle of this process. It's just like we were going down that path, and people were saying good things, positive things. I felt like I was driven to the ground, and then they would pick me up, like I cannot give up. When you see a vision, when you have that direction to do something important, you have to keep moving forward. Then there's times when you have to step back, and wait to hear what you need to do next.

It was a long haul. I would call Nelson and he would say, "Okay, let's leave this for a month or two." And I would say, okay. Then we would come up with another strategy, and then we would move on. I always had to keep working, because when I believe in something, even if I don't get paid to do it, I do it, because of my convictions. I always like to be there to follow through with what I'm here to do. So we would leave it for a while. I always give thanks to Nelson, even today.

I moved back to my house at Siksika in 1992. I had to move home to support some family members. I kept working on the shelter project for Calgary, but I wanted to do work at home, at Siksika, too. Strater Crowfoot was the Chief of Siksika and he was aware of my work in Calgary with the Shelter, violence against Native women, child welfare, and addictions. My sister- in- law, Mildred Scalp Lock and I met with Strater. Strater has always been a person that looked at the well-being of Siksika for the healing of the People. So, we got a place to work, and we worked with foster parents, and we also started working in the area of prevention of family and domestic violence. Women started coming to us. We used Elders and that program was called Kamotanni Centre, a Blackfoot word that means a place of safety, of survival and new birth. I still have that Band Council Resolution that supported it.

I had told Strater that I really had to go look at some of these shelters that served Native people. There was one up North and he said, by all means, I'll send you. So, I had my very first experience with riding the plane with a clear mind! I had to laugh. The reason I say that was because long ago I got picked up and was put in jail. I had a free ride from Calgary to Edmonton on a plane and my hands were cuffed. Back in those days if you were charged with being drunk, you were taken to Fort Saskatchewan Jail for twenty days. At the time it was sort of fun, just what you go through when you are in that state, living on the street and drinking. At the end they told you to keep your nose clean, gave you some tobacco and a bus ticket, and you headed back to start all over again.

Strater gave Mildred and I two plane tickets from Calgary to Edmonton and back. For me especially it was such a big thing to go on a plane ride. So we got to the Edmonton airport, and I felt, "This is really something." I'd never been in an airport. All these things were a big novelty and I enjoyed every minute of it. Then we had the chance to go for lunch, stayed at my girlfriend's place, even slept on the floor. I went to that shelter, and I'll never forget what the Director told me in that meeting. I told her in our shelter we are going to work with the whole family, the women, the men, and the children.

She told me outright, "You're crazy, it's not going to work." Then I kind of smiled and I sat back and I said, "Well you might think that way, but in our culture, our family is a circle. In my vision, I was told that you have to work with the whole family. If you just work with the women, it's not going to work. You have to work with the whole family, because we're all hurting – we all have pain. You take away the women, they come home. We don't want to separate the families, we have to keep the circle strong. "

But this lady didn't understand what I was saying. When I ran up against negative feedback, it just gave me more fuel.

I just laughed and I told her, "Thank you ever so much." I told her, "Thank you for telling me I'm crazy. One day it's going to work."

It took time for us to have it incorporated as a Board. We had our temporary office at the Native Friendship Centre in Chinatown. The Friendship Centre let us use an office, where we started support groups for women. We had absolutely nothing, no papers to write on, no pens, nothing. We just kept going. We were asking for donations, a few dollars here and there. We sort of bummed around to get money!

I needed to focus on spearheading the whole shelter initiative, in the role of Chairperson of the Board. We brought on Gerri Many Fingers to direct the development of the Shelter, to help raise funds and look for a site. Eventually, after all the hard work of everyone, and the volunteers, money started to come in. After a lot of negotiating and working with the City of Calgary, we finally got our first Shelter facility. It was on 10th Street in Sunnyside, part of the social housing company in Calgary. We had the whole three story apartment building, with an office on the main floor, and we had security.

About this time, my great aunt, Margaret Bad Boy, approached me.

I had known Margaret Bad Boy since I was a young child. She was a close relative of my Father. She was a big, strong woman from a successful ranching family. As a child I was afraid of her. That changed over time as I saw her at the Sundance and other ceremonies. I got to know her. She was watching me for many years, the work I was doing since I sobered up. Margaret was a proud woman, with great self-respect. She became like my Mother, my friend, my Grandmother, my Auntie, my everything. She was very compassionate. She was not soft spoken. You could hear her voice and she was strongly committed to our People. She must have thought I was ready.

She told me, "My Girl, it is time that you have a name, a special name, one that will help you in your work for our women. Back in 1930, me and my husband had a sacred shield transferred to us at a Sundance. It is Awo Taan, the Shield. Now I will give you this name, Awo Taanaakii, meaning Shield Woman. You will have the protection of the Shield. It will also shield the women you protect, and it will shield all who walk with you on your path."

I did see the shield, when my Great Aunt was still alive. It was so soft, and you could hardly see the paint on it, where they used the red ochre.

At the opening of the first Shelter, Reg Crowshoe, an Elder from Piikani, did the ceremony to give me my name. There was so many people there, Strater Crowfoot, the Siksika Chief, other Chiefs of Treaty 7, the Mayor of Calgary, Al Duerr, Barb Scott, Ralph Klein, the Premier of Alberta, and many other delegates. A group of young drummers gave us four songs, as four is a sacred number in our culture.

My name is sacred to me, and I carry it with pride and respect. I always think back to my great aunt and what she told me, that whenever something is transferred from one person to another, in our Siksika culture, it is very special, very sacred. Women need the protection I have in this name. My tipi also bears an image of the original shield on it.

In turn, I gave this name to the Aboriginal Women's Shelter, and the Shelter bears this name today, the Awo Taan Healing Lodge. The first Shelter location was only temporary, so we needed to look for a permanent place. We went back and we started negotiating again. We had community meetings at different places in Calgary. One meeting, in particular, I always remember. It was very political when we met with the community members.

This one woman got up and she said, "Well we don't want drunken

Indian men walking the streets all hours of the night looking for their women!"

We really had to explain that the police would be there if they came around the neighbourhood. We went into detail with everything, and I was so upset because there were so many politics, and racist things said in that meeting. I always remember that meeting. Of course I was just sitting there listening, and some members of our Board were there. I just sat there. I really learned to keep cool when I ran into these kind of situations.

So, after I heard these things I just got up and calmly told them, "Thank you very much. I do appreciate this meeting, and hearing your concerns." Inside, I was so frustrated and angry.

I could have got mad, but I thought to myself, that's going to defeat the purpose. They understood what they were saying, but they didn't listen to what we were saying.

Then the City was going to give us another place in an industrial area. We met with a representative of the Council of Calgary and I really got ticked off. I told him, you might as well send us to the Calgary Zoo! He understood what I was saying, and there was no way we were going to have the Shelter in an industrial area.

Another time, a rich business man wanted to give us a house in the Calgary "Big Shot" area. We would have to move it. It was a beautiful house. It had hardwood floors, had gold faucets in the bathrooms, big bedrooms, walk - in closets, you name it, a big beautiful home. But we couldn't get it because the people in the neighbourhood, they didn't want their trees to be cut down or whatever. They didn't want to damage that whole area I guess, so we didn't get that house. And, where are we going to move this house to? It was frustrating. Then there was an old school, Connaught School in Sunalta. We were told to go look at it to see if we wanted to use that old school. But, no way, that wasn't a place for women to go.

There was so much negotiating. Then we got our building finally. We worked a lot with Ralph Klein, the Premier, and many others from the City. I knew Ralph for a long time, and Ralph was always around to help us.

So, finally, after eight years of hard work, we had our Native Women's Shelter in Calgary. It still bears my name, Awo Taan Healing Lodge. I was the Chairperson for the longest time, but I couldn't keep it up because of my work with Chief and Council at Siksika. I would go over there once in a while to see how things were going. I would go whenever they would invite me, to speak on special occasions. I felt the importance for me to stay involved because they wanted me to support them and the issues, and for the history I had.

They had an established Board, they had good people on the Board, so I just didn't feel that I needed to be an active part of it at that point. Really, even today my heart is still in the Shelter. But now, the time that I have in my life, I need to focus on my people, my community, in Siksika.

# Sharing their stories

The following people graciously shared their
reflections with Jim

Bob Hawkesworth

Nelson Gutnick

Mary Jane Amey

June Wiggins

"I knew you were coming. I could hear you laughing
all the way from Calgary."

# shared stories: **Bob Hawkesworth**

*Bob Hawkesworth is a fixture of Alberta politics. He was a Calgary Alderman from 1980-1986, and from 1993-2010. He also served as a Member of the Legislative Assembly of Alberta (MLA), representing the New Democratic Party from 1986-1993. In 2000, he won a Spirit of Gold Award from the United Way for his role in co-chairing the Calgary Homeless Initiative. He is a true social progressive in our Province.*

*I spoke with Bob in his home in north Calgary where he shared his long personal connection with Ruth, ranging from their days of community work and into parallel paths of public service. They share a common commitment to social justice issues.*

---

I remember when I first met Ruth early in 1977. At the time, I was managing two projects, one the Indian Lutheran Race Relations Committee, the other a Native street worker project in Calgary. One of the folks I worked with was Roy Little Chief who was advocating for status First Nations people in the City. People who had come into Calgary from reserves were having a tough time, facing poverty, discrimination and lack of work. We were generally advocating for people who didn't have a voice and trying to use their Treaty status as a way of helping them access services.

Roy told me he had a couple of women he wanted me to meet. We met in a non-descript coffee shop in what is now the Grand Theatre. Ruth was one of them. Dorothy Melting Tallow was the other. They had both been sober for a while, not a long time, maybe a couple of years. At that time Roy and I were doing some community organizing. We talked about how they could get active in helping some of the services become more effective. Sometimes, it was about creating a little ruckus, shaking things up a bit. It wasn't always effective, but it was the start to some great friendships.

These were the early days. It seems like a long time ago. There was nothing in the City for urban Natives then and people were being denied services. There were a lot of issues about off - reserve Indians. Eventually, Treaty 7 services to people in Calgary came out of this kind of work - the agitation and confrontations that happened in the 70's. In the process I met these absolutely amazing people. Of all the people I met at that time in my life, I still maintain a relationship with Roy Little Chief and also with Ruth Scalp Lock. I had the honour of being a pallbearer at Dorothy's funeral. Even though I had not seen her for several years, her family contacted me through Ruth and said they wanted me to be her pallbearer. That touched me deeply.

Through her work teaching Life Skills, beginning as a coach at the Indian Friendship Center, she was able to offer people real learning and she could speak to it from her own personal experience. She was trying to help others get their life together. She was persistent and committed to it. I saw her leadership style developing. When she agreed to do something, she followed through on it. That was evident from an early point.

Then came her advocacy in developing a whole new set of services for women fleeing violence. She got that started in Calgary. It is where it first started, with Ruth.

I was kind of sad or disappointed that she went back to Siksika, because we were losing somebody I saw as a real leader, a hope, somebody who could take an idea and move with it and get things to happen here in Calgary. I recognized we were losing somebody important, and significant, but she felt the draw to go home. That was where her calling was. In retrospect that was where she needed to be and in the end I think it was probably the right place for her to go. But it was Calgary's loss.

When I was a New Democrat (ND) Member of the Legislature in 1992, there was a vacancy in the provincial Little Bow constituency, and there was a by-election. This was a huge rural area, with Siksika, Ruth's community, being only a small portion of it. I called Ruth and said, you know, the Little Bow constituency doesn't have a New Democrat candidate, would you be interested? That didn't take any effort on my part. I didn't need to cajole or charm or sweet talk her into it. She just said, okay, I can do that. She jumped at it.

I remember Ruth bringing out Elijah Harper in 1992. Elijah Harper was an elected Native member of the Manitoba Legislature, who is famous for holding up ratification of the Meech Lake Accord which prevented the Constitutional amendments going through. He did this while holding an Eagle Feather in the Legislature. He was unhappy with the lack of definition for First Nation Treaty rights and Aboriginal rights in the Constitution. So I remember Ruth inviting me to come out to Siksika for a rally with Elijah. That's the nature of the relationship she and I had. In that case she took the initiative and I worked with her to help organize that.

Elijah came to Siksika, very much seen as a champion. He was soft spoken and there was no rabble rousing to the barricades. He was not a demagogic speaker. He didn't use "barnburner" oratory skills. It wasn't that at all. He was more conciliatory, soft spoken. It seems he came partly to speak and partly to talk and listen. There wasn't a large crowd, but it was energetic and they listened intently. Ruth was the key activist who pulled the event together. She identified with the symbolism and the importance of his actions and felt compelled to show support and bring others to the cause.

These seemed to be events in her life that helped her see a gift, an interest, a passion for leadership. People, like myself, saw her as a leader in her community. And I think she began to realize she had a gift, and that she could step up to the mark.

As part of her campaign, I took her down to the high school in the small rural town of Vulcan, which is where I went to Junior High School. So we thought maybe we should go introduce our ND candidate and see what questions people had for her.

I picked Ruth up and we drove to Vulcan to meet people. We ended up in a classroom with all these young people. I think it was part of a civic engagement education for the high school students to interview the different candidates that were running.

Ruth just talked with them. I thought, gee, this is a woman who feels quite at home, confident and not apologetic. She's happy to talk about her life and her community, and listen to other people tell her what they think they need. It was one of the more interesting experiences of my life as an MLA, to go right into the heart of Social Credit country with Ruth Scalp Lock as our ND candidate.

I saw these qualities in her that came from all her experiences. She had lived in Calgary all these years. She knew what it was like to be First Nations, coping and advocating, racism and discrimination, but she had the strength of character not to be a victim, to have a positive attitude. She was going to do something about this and she could take people as they came. She didn't worry about these things.

At the end of the day, we drove back and I dropped her off at Siksika. After, I thought how well-spoken she was as a candidate. I was proud to be associated with her. I just thought she stepped up and did a wonderful thing, speaking in the role of a Provincial Government candidate. I just couldn't have asked any more of Ruth than what she gave.

It was an unusual setting and it was brave of Ruth, I think, to step forward. Part of it also highlighted the cultural, racial, social divide that exists in southern Alberta. She did okay in the election, but there was low turnout at Siksika. She did place third in the race. Our campaign didn't have a lot of resources and I think a lot of people in the ND Party had given up on the riding as a forgone conclusion, so they didn't really invest the time and effort that should have been invested to truly support Ruth. There's also this issue from the Aboriginal perspective, "are we undermining our Treaty rights and our special relationship with Canada by playing the white man's politics?" And "the province is not our jurisdiction, our jurisdiction is federal". So there's a certain reluctance, even amongst her own community, to really fully participate in the electoral process. There were huge barriers there.

Ruth had caught the elected politics bug. Sometime after, she decided to take a run for Band Council. Again, the issues she was working on continued to be social services, quality of life for children, educational opportunities, safety for women, economic opportunity for women - a set of issues the "old boy's network" wasn't really focused on. She had this set of values and being on Council was a way of advocating for those values.

I was always grateful whenever an election came around and saw that she was elected or re-elected. That went on for a lot of years. She had a good long run. I was very proud of her because it's not an easy thing to win election after election. You really do have to have a broad basis of support to keep going in that role. I think it's a credit to her.

Ruth has a strong will. I don't know very many people who would have the strength of will that Ruth has. I don't have any idea what it means to go every day for 38 years now without having a drink. I find coming home after a hard day's work or after a bit of a setback, it's easy to unwind with a glass of wine. It's easy to escape into self-pity. It's easy to be self-absorbed when you face a setback or don't have such a good day or something happens that upsets you a bit.

Then I think, well nobody has dumped on me because of my skin or the way I look, or my gender. Whatever issue I've had, it's not anywhere close to what I'm sure Ruth has felt. She's very empathetic, so when she sees other people hurt and down, I'm sure she takes it to heart. I just think of all the millions of little pressures of things that have probably emerged in her life. She can't reach for a bottle of wine, and won't do that. The self-discipline and the will to not give in, is something I don't even know how to imagine. I just feel that's something that I admire deeply.

One special part of Ruth is when she laughs. It is the most infectious laugh! Ruth has a slow, deliberate way of talking and you can be mistaken that maybe she's down or she's sad. But then, all of a sudden, she'll chuckle. It's a genuine chuckle. She sees something humorous in a situation and the point in the conversation takes on a different tone. She has a very positive, optimistic view of the world. Given everything she's been through, maybe that's the gift she gives herself and maybe that's how she manages to accomplish all she does.

Whatever test of character I've been through, it's not been the crucible that she's been forced to go through. The fact that she's come through on the other side as strong and beautiful a person as she is, is truly a gift, a real blessing, an amazing accomplishment.

I was very moved at the 35th anniversary of her sobriety. She made the comment that, had she not done this, she would be dead like all of her siblings... all but one. At times I believe I have no true idea the magnitude of what she's carrying as her life experience. I only have had the privilege of catching a glimpse of it from time to time.

So I'm honoured to know her. To be counted as her friend is very special for me.

# shared stories: **Nelson Gutnick**

*Nelson Gutnick worked for the Government of Canada, Department of Indian Affairs, for many years. He then taught at the University of Calgary for seventeen years. He was the first non-Aboriginal winner of the Chief David Crowchild Memorial Award. Nelson passed away in March 2014.*

*Nelson would have met Ruth in Calgary when she was about 25 years old. It was a time of ideals, authority was challenged, people were wanting change. It was important to stand up for what you believed in.*

*Nelson had a strong connection with Ruth, first personally as her supporter, then as her mentor with the Shelter. He was the "old man" walking with her in her dream. Nelson's approach wasn't about giving people what he thought they needed, it was about getting them to think about what they wanted in their lives. "Are you a rebel?" I asked him. He chuckled, "No…I'm just responsible, helping people to be responsible for themselves."*

*I smile when Nelson mulls, somewhat puzzled, over the meaning of Ruth's phone calls, decades later. Ruth wasn't going to forget this man who had helped her when he appeared in her dreams.*

———————————————————

I first met Ruth when I moved from Fort Qu'apelle, Saskatchewan to Calgary in about 1968. I had been the community development worker there and when that program disappeared I was moved to Calgary as Supervisor of Social Services with Indian Affairs.

Ruth was seeking social assistance while she was still having a problem with alcohol. I had arrived at a decision on my part that when people came in from the reserve they had a right to stay in the city. Previously the dialogue was along the lines of "how did you get here?" then "now find your own way back." The reasons people came was first of all to escape violence and Ruth talked a little bit about that, and then to get her children an education. Like many Aboriginal women at the time, she was looking for resources, opportunity, safety, and a new way to look at her life. She was beginning to realize she had something to contribute.

Ruth was one of many people who came, and it took a little while, without pushing her, exploring "why did you come here?" just to allow her to express herself. After a while she expressed concern about what was happening in her own life, for her children and her own personal being. I guess she felt comfortable coming to the office.

At one point I had gone to a training in Ottawa, and we were taught to be Community Development workers. The first day we got there, we sat around in a circle. The facilitator never said anything for an hour and nobody else said anything. All the people in the room were totally responsible for what took place for three months.

My approach is based on my understanding that people can make up their own minds in their own way, without me describing what they had to do and did not have to do. I continued to use that philosophy with all the people that came to the office.
No one had ever done that before. It was radical because Indian people would say, what is your program? I would say, "I don't have a program. Where do you want to go and what do you want to do?" Basically, that was my approach working with Ruth and others.

Because of my perspectives, I was not really that welcome with Indian Affairs policy makers. I was considered associated with the Aboriginal people, so sometimes I was not welcome into our administration office. I wasn't part of the "in" group.

Ruth worked for her people. Ruth's focus was to find people accommodation, visit Aboriginal people in the hospital, a very positive role. She was amongst a few other women who began to take a very positive role in the City and they felt they had something to contribute. She started to realize that she no longer should be involved with alcohol and found something worthwhile in her life that would give her some meaning.

Indian Affairs felt that I didn't fit in with their policy anymore. I guess I was too much of a thorn in people's side. I was very fortunate to get on with the University of Calgary in the Faculty of Social Work. I didn't apply, didn't fill out an application. I would never be hired today because I didn't have a Doctorate. I was told I was hired because I was willing to take a stand on important issues. If I hadn't had that I don't know what I would have done. We had four children.

Ruth's work was beginning to focus on women who were abused, and this lead to her inkling that she would like to have a Native Women's Shelter. This became her goal and it took a long, involved period of time. Several of us worked very closely with her, but it was always her goal, what she wanted to do. We would just help her to make it occur. Ruth was a quiet presence, unassuming. She knew what had to be done, and she found a way to do it.

I was on the Board for the Women's Shelter, so we used to meet quite frequently. Gradually I became less and less involved as other people themselves started to take over. Over time, I'd gone about as far as I could go with supporting the Shelter process. People gradually took over and my role just disappeared. I felt that they were on their way. I'd offered all that I could, by talking, being someone to listen to, accepting her the same as I accepted other people.

What I learned from Ruth was persistence. She had a very quiet way of getting things done, very unassuming, knew what had to be done and had to find a way to do it. It took a lot of work getting the Shelter going.

One thing I will always think of with Ruth...her phone calls, many years after I had any active involvement with her. When she had her 35th celebration of sobriety I was invited to go. She made a special point. She called me two or three times, "Are you coming?"

When my wife passed away, just a few years ago now, Ruth called. She phoned to say, "How are you?" Even three weeks ago, she phoned and said, "How are things going for you?"

She still remembers and still has enough faith that I did something... and so, she still calls.

# shared stories: **Mary Jane Amey**

Mary Jane first met Ruth in the mid 1980's when they worked together at the shelter. Mary Jane and Ruth speak affectionately and respectfully of each other. One senses a real kinship between them, and a belief that they were meant to know each other, that they were sharing the same path in some way. As with many of Ruth's relationships, they started in one place and lead to many others. The relationship starts in the shelter, and carries on to the windy plains on Ruth's campaign trail in South East Alberta.

Mary Jane is now retired and living in Quebec where she and her husband run a hobby farm, and raise a few pheasants.

I am drawn in by Mary Jane's story of her first encounter with Ruth, how Ruth entered her life, "it was magical."

---

I returned to University to take an after degree course in Social Work at the University of Calgary in January 1984. I had taught English as a Second language in Nigeria for 2 years in the mid -1970s and had 2 children by then. It did not take much time for me to realize that I was a "macro" focused social worker. I took any course on social policy that they offered, along with any and all courses on Aboriginal policy with Nelson Gutnick. I was particularly interested to learn that Aboriginal women across Canada had for decades struggled to maintain their Indian status when they "married out." One had even taken her case to the Supreme Court of Canada and the United Nations Human Rights Committee. I admired their perseverance and tenacity and their willingness to take political action. I also learned that once Indian bands controlled their own membership, it would be a step towards self-government. My African experience had indelibly influenced my perceptions on the adverse effects of colonialism and I was strongly supportive of gender-balanced Aboriginal self-government. With hindsight, I know now that with these studies an invisible thread was drawing me toward Ruth Scalp Lock.

In the fall of 1984, I began my first Social Work practicum at a women's shelter. Very quickly I realized that a large percentage of the women were Aboriginal and informed by my coursework, I worked very hard to understand their concerns and gain their trust. Once I graduated with my undergraduate degree in 1985, I returned to the shelter to work as the Volunteer Coordinator and soon became the Assistant Manager. I then approached the Director about my concerns for the Aboriginal women and proposed that we hire an Aboriginal counselor, as a step toward culturally sensitive service provision. She suggested that I write a proposal to that effect. I did so and the plan was accepted.

The very next day, by some unexplained coincidence, I answered the phone. It was Ruth Scalp Lock, who was doing cold calls to various human service organizations, looking for employment. She told me that she had worked on a certificate from Mount Royal College and did counseling. I finally asked her who her people were and learned that she was Blackfoot, from Siksika. I then told her why I was asking and we invited her in for an interview two days later. Somewhere during that conversation, Ruth and I had our first great laugh together. Dozens more occasions for laughter followed over the years, even though we worked on a very tough issue. Ruth was hired and for the shelter staff, our real education began.

At the shelter, most of the staff dressed in the shelter uniform: jeans, running shoes and T-shirts, with long sleeves in the winter.

Ruth on the other hand was a fashion plate. She arrived at work in dresses or matching blouse-skirt combinations, with a solid coloured jacket on top. Her nails were always perfectly manicured, her make-up professionally appropriate, and her hair carefully coiffed. I don't think I've ever seen a pair of running shoes on Ruth's feet! And yet, one day as we were driving together past the zoo, Ruth pointed over to a bridge we passed and said: "In my drinking days, I used to sleep under that bridge." I couldn't reconcile that mental picture with the beautifully turned out woman sitting next to me in the car. On another occasion she told me that she had learned to take care of her appearance at a Life Skills course she took shortly after she stopped drinking. It changed her life. By the time I met her, she wasn't bitter about what she learned or didn't learn from the nuns in residential school. Amongst other things, for modesty sake, she had been required to shower with her shirt on.

On occasion at the shelter, I would fill in for an absent counselor and do counseling, instead of administration. I was always delighted when I could work with Ruth and June Wiggins. We seemed to have a creative synergy and tackled all the issues of communal living in a shelter with as much humor as we could muster. Crying babies, dirty laundry and women returning to abusive partners were more tolerable together.

It seemed a natural progression for Ruth to move on to planning for the building of a Native women's shelter. She called on all her old colleagues and friends. I was recruited to coach non-researchers on how to do a Needs Assessment, as this was required before anyone would even talk about funding. It was a time of ups and downs, and I recall one of the low times was when the attractive Awo Taan logo, given to Ruth by her late grandmother, was stolen from a car. Eventually Ruth had met with all the elected officials, bureaucrats, and funders and the shelter was to be reality. We both stood together and wept during the ceremony to open the temporary shelter on 10th Street in 1993.

For me, Ruth is synonymous with being an advocate for Aboriginal women, especially those in violent situations. It was Ruth who pointed out that Aboriginal women have a double burden. They are not only victimized by men within their own communities, but are preyed upon by mainstream men as well. Some of the most aggravated assaults happened to Aboriginal women. I don't think I ever heard Ruth refer to herself as a feminist but she certainly promoted equality for women.

Ruth is also a strong politician. I can't remember the time-frame when Ruth ran for the New Democrats in the provincial riding of Little Bow but it was before she decided to assume leadership at Siksika. During that campaign I canvassed for Ruth on two occasions in small prairie towns in the riding. Racism was not overt but many times I was asked: "Is she an Indian?" Ruth learned probably more than she wanted to know about mainstream politics through that experience. On election night when results came in, Ruth had gained all the Siksika-Gleichen votes and very few in the rest of the riding. The courage it takes to put yourself forward in such a way is phenomenal.

I remember one time we were having coffee in North Hill Mall and Ruth told me she wanted to become a leader for her people. She had heard of a man in the Navajo nation down south who was holding "vision quest" type workshops in the US and she was planning to attend. She needed some kind of sign that pursuing a leadership role was right for her. I encouraged her to test herself in that way. Several weeks later we were back in the mall and she said: "I'm not cut out to be a spiritual leader of my people; I'd be better as a political leader." She explained how the workshop had helped her come to that realization. Several months later she ran for Band Councilor at Siksika and has served many terms.

The last time I saw Ruth was at Bob Hawkesworth's campaign office for his final run for City Alderman in Fall 2007. I noticed on that visit that Ruth, who balanced between the city white world and the Native reserve world, was definitely more attuned to and connected to her reserve. We still took the opportunity on that occasion to discuss whether Ruth should have had a perm as well as colouring her hair and whether I should stop highlighting mine now that the silver was starting to show—our "girl" talks were definitely the best!!

Ruth taught me so much about her culture, about working across cultures (ask questions, don't assume), about persevering through adversity and trying new things. Ruth's greatest strength was her ability to mobilize people to work towards realizing her vision.

She taught me about the importance of taking care of herself and most of all... that laughing is the best medicine.

# shared stories: **June Wiggins**

*June Wiggins is an old friend and colleague of Ruth's. She is now retired and living in Cochrane. She is still connected to the Aboriginal community in Morley. Her daughter is a teacher who has an interest in First Nations, which June attributes to Ruth, "Ruth sort of gets you interested in what's going on."*

*June and Ruth shared many experiences, starting in the mid 1980's. Working together in a women's shelter in Calgary, Ruth would have been about 40 years old when they met, living in Calgary and Siksika with her two children. It was during this period that Ruth's vision for a Native wowen's shelter began to take shape.*

*June struck me as a "real" person, down to earth, the kind that Ruth becomes friends with easily. Her perspective on the unique needs of Aboriginal women is clear, as is her description of Ruth's way of getting people involved: "She talks, a lot, you listen, and then you're hooked and you're helping out!" For June, Ruth comes across as a real character, from a different world in a way, and a great companion. I was enthralled with June's stories that find her in the Aboriginal world. These stories bring their experiences to life, and are marked by her wonderment at some of the strange, inexplicable things that occurred, "It happened, who's to say how? It just did."*

---

I met Ruth when I was in University in 1986-87. I was a struggling student and I did a practicum placement at the shelter, then I was hired to work there part time. Ruth generally worked the 3-11 shift with me, and she would tell stories. That was her big thing and Ruth's got a way of telling a story that goes on and on and on, and then suddenly you get the point. She told a lot of stories about her Dad and the reserve. She has got an uncanny ability to get people on board, to sell an idea.

It was Ruth's idea to start a Women's group out of our outreach program. I did my Masters Project in this group. It all started with Ruth talking about issues, like basically telling us what it was like when she was growing up.

The group with the Native women was incredible. It was standing room only. I remember we had 24 kids in child care one night. Doing that group was so cool because we never knew who was going to walk through the door. The first thing the group members would do is figure out who the new woman was. Every time a new member came to the group, the women somehow knew a cousin or somebody that was related to them. It's a small community in a lot of ways.

I remember funders came in to watch us because they couldn't believe we had this group going. The women were really gung-ho, really cool, because it was a real social thing for them. We'd do the sweet grass, the whole bit. The groups usually started off with Ruth telling a story from her experience. Then it would just take off from there. Like, once I remember her putting her feet up on the table and saying, "and that's another thing, the shoes they made us wear at school, it ruined my feet!" So then, other women would join in and tell a story. A lady from up North told how, when she was at Residential school there, some kids came in from farther away. These kids traditionally wore shells under their shoes to keep their feet dry. At the school, they weren't allowed to do this, and they were never comfortable this way.

They were really enthusiastic because it was something that they wanted and that they needed. When we did groups with the Natives and the white women, it didn't go over well, because the Native women were very quiet. It was really evident at the shelters too, that the Aboriginal women did not mix with the white women. It was just really noticeable. They were very careful which staff they talked to, because they didn't know if the staff could relate to them culturally.

But when they had their own group they were very vocal. The stories that they told were incredible. A lot of them related back to residential schools. I remember one group was talking about women going missing on the reserves. It was almost every one of them had an aunt or a cousin that they had never heard from again. They talked a lot about what it was like in residential school, and it was amazing how they helped each other. The older kids helped the younger ones to learn to speak English, just to get by.  That was the big thing.

There was a need to understand cultural issues or why they were doing things differently. For example, they take on kids. It could be the sister's kid, but they'll take the kid and that'll be their kid, but it's really not their kid. So you can get a woman that shows up with 7 or 8 kids, but she's only 24, and she says they're all her kids. So it's this whole thing of family.

The mothers were very gentle with their kids, the way they spoke to them. With the women, they have different ideas about rules. If you don't have your kids in bed at a certain time, that wouldn't be a priority. There were a lot of issues that would come up that we as counselors didn't quite get, and we probably offended them. But Ruth was always telling us what it was like on the reserve and that's the way it was.

That sort of gentle persuasion that Ruth has, I think Ruth basically educated all the counselors on a lot of the First Nations issues.  As part of the process, she was going on and on about how they needed a shelter. I think that one by one she started selling us on this idea. So we all sort of, "Yup, it's a good idea Ruth."

We had applied for funding for a position to lead a needs assessment. Mary Jane Amey was a rocket scientist at research. Ruth doesn't have a background in research and all this stuff, but Ruth's got an ability to get people on board. She was able to bring people together through telling stories and pointing out that this was a real need. So I think all the workers knew there was a need, but we had to go to the community and build a case.

Ruth had a cousin or member of her family come up with a logo and they had a TV that they were going to use to raise money by trying to sell tickets on it. One of the husbands of one of the woman that was in the group got wind of this and stole the logo and the TV. It was like someone got wind of these women getting "uppity," trying to get a shelter and the logo and this TV were stolen. It was an incredibly powerful group, but then the group disbanded, because I think there was a lot of fear.

I remember some stories from my times with Ruth.

Ruth's uncle, Alex, was a dancer. He danced worldwide. He worked at the Glenbow Museum in Calgary. The Glenbow had a show called "the Spirit Sings" for the 1988 Winter Olympics, showing Aboriginal masks from all over Canada. Some Aboriginal Elders thought they shouldn't ever be shown. They were too sacred. There was quite a bit of controversy on the news.

Alex died suddenly of a heart attack after being involved with this. Ruth had a hard time letting go of his spirit. Mark Wolf Leg was a medicine man at Siksika at the time. He put on a pipe ceremony, a high ceremony in their culture. A friend and I were the only two white women that were asked out there. I remember it was the wintertime and it was out on the reserve. It was all these old Elders, all these old ladies on one side and the old guys sitting on the other side. Maggie Black Kettle was out there. It was in a house. It was really cool because they passed the pipe around. Everybody had to bring something. I brought sandwiches, but there was pemmican out there and a lot of traditional things. The Elders all take an ice cream pail, and the ice cream pail was sitting next to them and what they didn't eat they just put in there and they take it home.

This pipe ceremony was really interesting. It was done in Blackfoot, but the leader was translating every now and then for my friend and I. Then he brought the spirits and he said that nobody can look up because bad things happen all the time if this ceremony went wrong. So at that time we were looking down. We weren't going to look up! All of a sudden I hear, "You can tell the white ladies they can look up now."

When we left there was an old lady who gave me a Native name. She asked Ruth if we'd come over and have tea at her place after. Now this was at night and I was living in Calgary. She told me I was the spirit of her mother. So, who am I to say? So going back we had the Elder with us, she was sitting in the back with my friend. I was driving and Ruth was sitting in the front. It was getting dark out and snowing. An eagle got in my headlight and it was flying back and forth and it did this for about half a mile. It was just amazing.

I'm sitting in the front and I said to Ruth, "Do you see that?" and Ruth very quietly said, "It's my uncle." I had never seen anything like that in my life. It was his spirit leaving I think.

Here is another story that happened when I was with Ruth.

Mary Jane Amey was the head of an important committee in Calgary and it got quite political, and Mary Jane's stress level was getting up there. So, Ruth decides that Mary Jane needs to go to a Medicine Man for some healing. I had recently fallen taking the garbage out and broke two of my ribs and could barely move, so Ruth felt I should go along too. So Mary Jane and I go up to the reserve again and meet with this Medicine Man. We drove in separate cars, Ruth by herself, and me and Mary Jane together. Well, it turns out that Ruth hadn't even called him and told him we were coming out. It was like, why bother? We get in there and he looks at Ruth and he says, "I had a dream. I knew you were coming because I could hear you laughing all the way from Calgary. I knew you were bringing two white women with you."

This guy took us into this little room and he did something to my back. It was like pulling the guts out. I could barely move, so Mary Jane drove on the way back.

We stopped in at the truck stop coming back in from Gleichen. We went to the bathroom. We were looking at our backs to see if we had a hole in them, if we were bleeding. Well, what the hell was that all about? I mean those things you just can't explain, right? But I had no pain after that. It was weird. I had two broken ribs!

I've got one more story I would like to share. We're sitting at the shelter one night and the women were in bed and Ruth would be going on and on telling stories about her dad. We were talking about Neil Armstrong landing on the moon, and I was talking to her about my dad, because my dad passed away. He was quite elderly and he didn't quite believe they had landed on the moon.

Ruth was telling me about her dad and she said she'll never forget sitting on the couch watching them land on the moon with her dad. And her dad looked at her and he said "Do you think they seen Jesus?" It struck me as a really interesting combination of images, Jesus and the Great Spirit, the Moon, together. It just struck me that this was the old man, adapting the beliefs of the Church with his traditional beliefs. I will never forget that story.

Thinking about Ruth, she has got charisma, a real charm about her. She is the Tina Turner of the Native world, the way she dresses and everything. I remember people would say, "Where does she get the money?" She didn't have a lot of money, but Ruth has always carried herself well. And her laugh is absolutely infectious. She has an uncanny ability to connect with people too.

Ruth is such a leader in some ways. She's not really "the top leader." She's sort of right underneath the top, but she is a leader, and she gets people working. She sells them on an idea. It's her legacy, it's what she's left behind. Hopefully younger women will look at that and aspire to be like that.

I think that's how she's impacted so many people... her gentle persuasion.

# Part IV

# Adopted Relatives

"How could she be your sister, and you're the Premier?"

# Chapter 7 Ralph, blue bird

*Ralph Klein needs little introduction. Recently passed on, he is a legend in Alberta. To be sure, he had the common touch among Albertans, and to them he will always be "Ralphie." Ralph was born and raised in Calgary. Originally a television reporter, and then Mayor of Calgary, Ralph entered Provincial politics, and became Premier of the Province from 1992 until 2006. He established many friendships among the Siksika people.*

---

When Ralph Klein was a young reporter back in 1972, he got to know some of our people in Calgary and many of us became friends with him.

He was well liked at Siksika, and then he started learning the language too. He got to know Adrian Stimson, who was the Tribal Administrator. Ralph would come out to the pow wow, and sometimes he would be at the Indian Days.

I was adopted by Jim Many Bears and his wife Alice when I was fourteen. They were related to my family, and my mother wanted them to take care of me when she left this world. The old man, Jim, he was really good to me. He wanted things for me, to finish Grade 12, eventually leave the Reserve, to get a job and an education. He got to know Ralph and would have Ralph visit him in his tipi at the Indian days. That's how I met Ralph personally. As it turns out, Ralph and I were both adopted by Jim Many Bears. The old man had a naming ceremony for Ralph at his tipi. He was given the name Blue

Bird. Ralph was so excited about his name.

Jim Many Bears really cared for Ralph and Ralph just adored the old man. Maybe he never had a Father. Sometimes I think Ralph was really part Indian. Maybe he never disclosed or accepted, but I think he was. I could be wrong, but he was well liked and he really spoke the language. So that's how I got to know him.

When our Father, Jim Many Bears, passed away, both Ralph and I were named in the obituary as his adopted son and daughter. So we were like siblings in the traditional way.

My friends in Calgary, the ladies I worked with at the shelter, used to tease me, "Ruth, how's your brother Ralph Klein?" We would all laugh.

Over the years, I always had contact with Ralph. When I ran for the New Democrats in 1992, the rapport we had wasn't the same. I guess that was because I represented the New Democrats and he was with the Progressive Conservative party, so politically they are different. It upset me. I guess that's politics. It gets in the way of personal relationships.

First of all he was a reporter, then the Mayor of Calgary. I was working on the "Spirit Sings" at the Glenbow Museum in Calgary, and there were times he would come to the Glenbow to visit. He was very receptive, very warm, and we went and had lunch with him. He was always good that way. He would call me "sis," like being siblings in the Indian way.

When we were looking for government support for our Shelter, we had a meeting with Ralph, the Premier, and some of our group of supporters. I always remember Ralph at that meeting. We were meeting with him in this big room with some of his people, talking to him about our needs. We had talked with him many times and you could tell he was tired of hearing about it. Finally he slapped his hand on the table, making a loud noise. He said he was really frustrated and he really understood what we were going through. He said it in such a manner, like, it's about time you people start funding my sister's shelter. So let's get this thing going! Then I really felt that connection was there again. He really understood what I was going through. I knew that he wanted our women to have a place to go to, and to work for the whole family, the children and the men.

There was a World Indigenous Women's Conference in Calgary about 5 years ago. Ralph was one of the moderators on this panel and I was one of the speakers. That was when I felt that genuineness from Ralph, that he was my brother. I knew because he was so happy to see me. When we started the opening he said "I'd like to introduce my sister, Ruth Awo Taanaakii, who is here." He greeted everyone in different languages, Blackfoot, Cree, Tsuu T'ina, and all these other native languages. I felt good and we had a chance to talk. Then we were teasing each other. I asked him, do you still go out to Siksika, and he said, no, that was long ago. I asked him, what are you doing now? He said he was doing some private work, some consulting, and his wife was quite involved in the Native programs in Calgary. So they were still involved in some way. So that was my last good visit with him.

Of course Ralph got sick. He got sick and passed away. It really bothers me he went like that, because this man was so good, he was down to earth, a very caring man, and he's out to help anybody. I really feel bad about it.

I always feel that he was part of us. He was adopted by Siksika, so he's an honorary member. To me, Ralph is another Siksika member. The colour of a person to me doesn't mean anything.

When we had our 125th commemoration of the Treaty, at Blackfoot Crossing, my granddaughter Dana was still going to the elementary school at Crowfoot School in Cluny and Ralph was still the Premier. The students were brought to the Treaty flats. Dana, she's really outgoing, and Ralph was there and I was around too. I didn't even know Dana was talking to Ralph and she brought Ralph to our tipi and asked him to come inside.

Dana introduced herself to him, "I'm Dana Stone Child. You know my grandmother Ruth Scalp Lock." "Who?" "Ruth Scalp Lock." "Oh yeah, my sister, where is she?" "She's over there somewhere." Dana gave him the whole historical background of our tipi, the Shield and the name, how we got the name, how we got the design. Ralph was so impressed. I got a chance to talk to him because we were going to have a feast at the grounds. He said "I met your granddaughter, Dana, she's something else Ruth. She explained the whole meaning of the tipi and the design".

He was really impressed with my granddaughter. He told Dana, "Your grandma's my sister, your grandma's my friend". And she said to Ralph, "How could she be your sister, and you're the Premier?"

I guess Ralph laughed and said "Well, ask your grandma and she'll explain that connection."

# Introducing **Theoren Fleury**

Theoren Fleury, better known as Theo, #14 to his fans, is a legendary hockey player in Canada and beyond. Theo was born and raised in Manitoba, and as a boy, hockey became his life.

As a hockey player, he is probably best known as a Calgary Flame, where he played from 1989 to 1999, winning a Stanley Cup in his first season. His rink- length slide after an overtime goal in Edmonton captured it all: Theo was "every kid" who had ever tried on skates with a dream of the Big Leagues, small but with the heart of a lion, bursting with enthusiasm and the cold-air spirit of the game. He was the fiery sparkplug of the Flames.

In 2010, Theo released his autobiography, Playing with Fire, where he tells of his upbringing, his hockey career, his abuse at the hands of his Coach Graham James, his struggle with addiction, and his recovery and healing.

Theo now spends a lot of time campaigning for awareness of the sexual abuse of children, their rights and needs as victims, or "victors" as he prefers to call them. He is also determined to impact the Justice system for the accountability of offenders. Theo speaks extensively to Aboriginal youth on the importance of having dreams and overcoming their challenges.

Theo is Aboriginal on his Father's side. His Grandmother, Mary Fleury, was Cree.

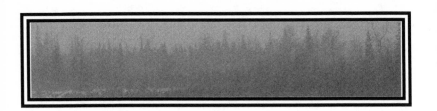

## Chapter 8 Theoren, the gently falling snow

The very first time I met Theoren Fleury was out at the Theo Fleury Hockey School in Calgary in the mid - 1990's. This was when my grandson Shawn Scalp Lock was playing minor hockey. We used to take some kids up there for the summer hockey school. At first I found Theoren to be kind of hard to connect with. I told him about it, but it took years I guess for him to really start coming out of himself. But at that time, when I met him, I kind of felt that barrier. I didn't blame him, because he didn't grow up with Native people, in a Native community.

When I met him he wasn't with the Flames anymore, he was traded to an American team.

So I got to know him and he would stay in touch with us, maybe a Christmas card, especially with my grandson Shawn. We had these pictures that were taken at the hockey school and he had a nickname for Shawn. He called Shawn "Bone Crusher" because my grandson is pretty big and he was way bigger than Theoren. "I wouldn't want to meet Shawn in a back alley," he said jokingly. It took time for us to get to know each other.

It's interesting. My grandmother was a Fleury, married to my Grandfather, Edward Butterfly. My mother was Cree. Those things I am very proud of today. Theoren's mother was also Cree. So maybe Theoren and I are related somehow.

When Theoren was with the Chicago Blackhawks I went to watch the game in Calgary.  They played the Flames and he recognized me and my niece and I didn't sit too far from the players bench.  I had on a Chicago Blackhawks jersey, and all these fans of the Flames, they really got after me. Theo threw this puck my way, to take as a souvenir. He was really acknowledging us, but these fans were really putting us down. They were just cussing and swearing, like it is so inappropriate for these people to behave that way. Not my way. Of course I was just laughing, and I told one of these guys I should have brought my hand drum and had a big pow-wow here! It was so hilarious. It was good.

Theoren was always in my visions, in my dreams, and I knew at some point in time he would be in my circle. I knew this young man needed someone to walk with him; he really needed somebody, because he didn't really have grandparents, or a matriarch, somebody to really teach him the way.

I went to watch him in Edmonton when he was with the New York Rangers. It was around the time of 9/11. I really wanted to see him. I took a cab right to the Coliseum and I purchased a ticket from one of the scalpers and that game was so funny.  Of course I had a New York Rangers jersey. Whenever I went to these games I wore Theoren's jerseys. Of course I had people making fun of me. I sat quite a way up, close to the nosebleeds, so I didn't really get a chance to catch Theo's eye.

I didn't see him again until he came back to Calgary and he had this flooring business, really fancy floor business.  I got a hold of the number, and then left a message. His wife Jennifer called.  So Jennifer and I spoke a long time on the phone, and I told her who I was. She said, "Oh, just come on down." So I went down and walked in. We met and he was so happy to see me. Theoren just knew, he always remembered me, from the hockey school and all those times I went to his games.  So, that is how we connected. That is how it all started.

He was so happy to meet me.  I really felt the warmth. It was different from that first contact, because back then I could just feel that he was kind of nervous when you first met him.

He told me that he was back in Calgary and at some point he would tell me the reasons for moving back to Calgary. He wasn't playing in the National Hockey League. He was on leave because I think he had to go for treatment. We didn't talk about it right then and there because there were some other people at the store.

It took time for him. I think he had to build that trust for me. Maybe he didn't really know that he could trust me because he was hurt so many times in the past. I was always kind of waiting, thinking one day he was going to come forward. I never rushed him. I never asked him too many questions. I just explained where I was coming from and why I was so concerned about his well-being. Then he started to talk about his problem with alcohol and drugs.

Eventually Theoren came out to Siksika and took part in the Sweat Lodge Ceremony. This really helped him get started in his healing journey.

We had this birthday for him out at our house in Siksika, about 5 or 6 years ago. We pitched up the tipi and he paid for all the steaks and hamburger. We had a lot of people come out and he stayed in a tipi with Jennifer. We had it on a Saturday, his birthday, the end of June that year. That was the first time he ever stayed in a tipi and he was helping me barbeque the meat, and he started crying. He had tears in his eyes. I asked him, "What's the matter, what's wrong?" He said, "I think my relatives, my ancestors were in this territory before, long ago." That is when I think it started to hit him, being Aboriginal, for him to go back, and fully accept it and do something with it.

That Sunday we had breakfast at our house. He said that was the first time he ever had a good sleep, with the fresh air, to be in the tipi. There were some friends that stayed in the tipi with them. Then we had the Round Dance, we had the youth, we had the

Elders. Oh it was fun. We really celebrated. I bought the birthday cake, we had gifts from these Elders, even pemmican, dried meat. They just appreciated him being out to Siksika.

I adopted him as my Grandson. I was told in a vision, that this young man never had a grandmother that was very close to him, that nurtured him, so I took that role as his Grandma, to teach him the way. Also my husband adopted him as his Grandson.

He said that he never knew a Grandmother and a Grandpa. He never had that time to be with his Grandparents.

That Summer we came up with his name. The naming ceremony took place that same year in August, down at the pow wow arbor. We pitched up our tipi. I asked these ladies to help me cook the meal and we had about 300-400 plates. When you are going to have a name, you have to be captured. Back in the day it was the warriors that captured you. These days, a veteran does this role. So my husband Francis, who is a veteran, performed that ceremony. First the warrior, my husband, danced around the circle four times. Then he "captures" the person to be named. Then Francis and Theoren together dance around the circle. Then something sacred happened. Behind my husband and my Grandson, Theoren, I saw two spirits following them, dancing. I cried when I saw this. We had an Elder who painted Theoren's face and sang holy songs, and there was a ceremony where Theoren was given his headdress. Now, he can wear his Head Dress at any pow wow, or any kind of celebration. That is how he got his name, the name Gently Falling Snow, iikinopotah. This is a name that came to me over time. It reflects the changes I saw in Theoren, from angry to softer, like the snow that falls gently, cleansing the soul, and the Earth.

It is a very special relationship that we have with Theoren, because he really takes me as his Grandma, and he has a lot of respect. He has mentioned that, for him, it is really special. He takes it as sacred. Going back to find his roots, maybe he never had that before. We met his parents, Walter Fleury, when they came to Calgary and we have been invited to go to Theoren's when they have a Christmas dinner. Walter, he gave us thanks and he really appreciated that we adopted Theo, knowing that he has that support here in Calgary.

Theoren is really making steps forward. He goes to the Sweat Lodge down on the Blood Reserve and he has been to sweats down here at Siksika. He speaks to the youth now. His message is about abuse, alcohol, the importance of education, to do something about your issues, your hurt and your pain.

Five years ago, that was when he really started with his healing.

# shared stories: **Theoren Fleury**

Theoren Fleury met Ruth when she brought some kids to Theoren's hockey school in Calgary. What they found, over time, was that they connected on many levels.

I met with Theo in his home, where he shared his story about Ruth and her impact on him. We talked about a lot of things, his new music career, and of course hockey. Theo showed me some pictures and awards from his career. He showed me his Head Dress, and the wooden box where he keeps his smudge. But mostly, I was struck by his honesty around his inner journey, and how Ruth gently helped his awakening. It is a unique and special relationship. Theoren described Ruth this way, "She gets it. So many don't get it. Just the meaning of life. Period."

---

Ruth used to bring a bunch of kids from Siksika to my Hockey School in Calgary. Her and I became fast friends. As an Aboriginal Indigenous person I always respected the Elders, and she was just kind of a neat lady. I thought at the time that it was important for us to have some Aboriginal kids at the school.

This hockey school turned out to be one of the best things I ever did. I've been to many hockey schools in my day and I've been to good ones and I've been to terrible ones and I knew what the time commitment was going to be. Thank god I was young. Really what made the hockey school special was that I was there all day every day. I was on the ice. My goal as the face of the school was to try and connect with each kid once every day.

So it was quite an undertaking but it ended up being a very successful school and we had people come from all over the world to this school. So it was nice to have some Aboriginal kids involved, so they could see something different, and get some really good coaching at the same time.

It was Ruth who brought these kids out. She just showed up out of the blue. Little did I know she was a big Fleury fan and a big Calgary Flames fan, and that's initially how I think the conversation started. But then after that she was at the rink all day every day. I would see her and we would have conversations and we became friends. She kept doing it year after year after year.

After that I saw Ruth very intermittently. It's not like we were in contact every week or anything. She told me her story of her struggles and at that time I was right in the middle of my addictions. She had a rough life, a hard life, and I respected the fact of where she was at that point in her life. I know from growing up with my parents through their addictions, I know how difficult it is to get clean and sober, but with Ruth I know once she got it, the world really opened up for her. She became this incredible role model for many, many people and has helped many people in her day. I really respect that about her.

I just love her demeanor. I think anybody who meets Ruth would be attracted to the serenity that she has. Anybody who's an addict, that's what they talk about - serenity. I know for the first few times I tried to get sober, there was absolutely no serenity happening. The way Ruth talks is really calm. She really thinks about what she's going to say before she says it. She's just one of those cool, respected Elders that everybody talks about. Now, what I do on a regular basis is travel around Canada speaking to different Aboriginal communities. Everybody knows Ruth.

Ruth has had an incredible influence on my spirituality. She's been my spiritual teacher, my spiritual leader. She's kicked me in the ass when I needed it. She makes sure I'm accountable when it comes to what I do today. She's really somebody that it's good to have on your side, because I think she has a direct line to the Creator. I think most people who have struggled with addictions can listen to her story and kind of get an idea of how you can achieve long term sobriety. Most people can stop drinking. Most people can stop the behaviour, but you know the drama, the insanity, all those things in your life will happen until you find spirituality.

Once you find spirituality, that's when you have long time, meaningful sobriety. They say in the program, its attraction not promotion. I think most people are attracted to Ruth because of that serenity that she has. I know that I was attracted to her demeanour and the way she spoke and the interesting way that she told stories. It kind of reminded me of my own Grandmother who passed away when I was 9 or 10. So I never really had that Aboriginal influence from my Grandmother. But there was a lot of similarities in the two that I saw.

Meeting Francis, Ruth's husband, my Grandpa, and listening to their stories of when they were in their addictions. It's wild stuff. I can totally relate to the insanity of the disease. But to see them today is pretty amazing. They're not getting any younger, but they're not getting any older either. They've found an enjoyment and fulfilment in life that, when you meet Ruth, that's what you're attracted to. You've seen this lady who's lived a hundred lives, but she's really, I think, enjoying her life today more than she has at any point.

After I got traded from Calgary I didn't spend a lot of time in Calgary during the summer. So we lost contact. I moved back to Calgary in 2004-05 and we opened up a decorative concrete business in Calgary. We were all sitting around at the end of one day and in walks Grandma Ruth. I was newly sober and I had just married Jen. We kind of picked up right where we left off.

I don't know if this was calculated or not but she started to encourage me to come out to Siksika and start working with the youth, and start telling people my story and what not. I was looking for that spirituality. I'd been looking for it forever. I grew up as an altar boy on Sunday in the Catholic Church and on Thursdays I was going to my Mom's Jehovah's Witness Bible study, so my concept of this higher power... it was nuts. It was nothing, right? It was all about guilt and shame and punishment and I didn't want any part of it.

I remember this one old timer coming up to me at some AA meeting in Santa Fe, and saying, how are you doing with your higher power stuff, and I was like, I have no clue what that looks like. And he said to me, in this program we get to pick our own God, and I was like, what are you talking about, because I only know organized religion – to the Nth extreme.

But I thought about it and I was like, yeah, I like that better than this other stuff. And so, because I was Jehovah's Witness, I never celebrated by birthday as a kid. My Dad went to Catholic Church and my mom went to Jehovah's Witness. I don't know how they made that work, but they did and they still do to this day. It was shortly after Ruth came back into my life that she said, "I'm going to have a birthday party for you at Siksika." And I said, "Cool, that'd be great."

So we drove out to Cluny, to her house and they have a bit of a driveway as you're pulling in, and there was a whole bunch of these logs that were just massive, long and a bit of cloth or material beside. I got out of the car and Francis was bringing the horses in, and I was like, "What's that over there?" He said, "That's a tipi, and we waited for you to help us set it up." I remember setting it up and putting it all together and then went to a Sweat Lodge at Brian's house, Francis' son, for the first time.

I remember not really knowing anything about sweats or what happens or anything. I went and did this sweat, and for the first time in a long time, spiritually I felt like I was home. I just remember being in the sweat and Clement, the leader - he was in there. He could visibly feel that I was uncomfortable in the sweat and he just kind of leaned over and said, "Just let it go." I'd been carrying around so much shit for so many years. It was very comforting. I did my best to let it go, and I remember leaving that sweat a different person. This was all orchestrated by Ruth. I didn't have a clue what was going on.

I met a guy named Arnold Mountain Horse who is one of the most powerful medicine men in the world. He lives in Cardston. I've been to his sweat several times. Along my travels, whenever I can sweat, I sweat. I've sweated with the Ojibway, the Denes, the Cree, the Metis, the Blackfoot, the Blood. My spirituality has been built on that.

It's just been incredible to be a part of that. I know I'm Metis and I'm not Blackfoot, but there's a sense of calm that's come into my life that was never there before, and a lot more understanding. So I've become this person who the Aboriginal community respects because of this attachment to this spirituality that I have. When I speak to communities I talk about my relationship with Ruth and how important the Elders are to the youth, because there's this big push now for the youth to not go down that road of drugs, alcohol, gambling, sex, food, you name it. They actually listen to me, because whenever I'm in communities I like to spend a few minutes with the Elders, to say, "What do you think I need to do, what do I need to speak about when I'm here?."

I remember doing a few speeches at the beginning in Native communities and it was just a shit show, and I'm like freaking out, because I'm like, where do I start? But Grandma Ruth says, "One at a time, just help one person at a time," and that made perfect sense to me. That's all you can do, instead of being overwhelmed with all the social issues and abuse. She said if one person hears you speak, the light goes on and that's all you can do. That made perfect sense, and it has evolved to where I'm very trusted in the Aboriginal community by everyone. They look to me because everybody knows where I was and where I am today.

We lack role models like Ruth and Francis and nobody knows about these people. There's Ruths' and Francis' in every community, but nobody celebrates that fact, nobody talks about it. To be honest, I think the whole Aboriginal community in Canada has to come to terms with the Residential Schools. Well, you know I was there myself, I had all kinds of issues, my parents weren't there for me, I was abused by my coach... you know. I had all these built in things in my life. But what happened is, and Ruth shared with me her rock bottom, am I going to allow this to define who I am for the rest of my life, or am I going to get up and dust myself off and save my own life?

All I can do is live by example. I can't preach, I can only share my own personal story and if it fits with people and if it gets them out of their chair and they can relate to my story, that's all I can do. That's all Ruth did for me, was share her experience, strength and hope with me. I was attracted to that, and I took the cotton out of my ears and put it in my mouth and here I am today. I have a great life, a great partner, I have great kids. That wasn't the case long ago. They didn't want to be in the same room with me. Ruth's story is important, especially in the Aboriginal community, to know that these people have had success. They haven't had to commit suicide. They've been able to find their niche in this world and that's important.

With Ruth, there's no judgment, because she's been there. When she told me the story of living on skid row in Winnipeg, I didn't see that in Ruth. I didn't see the insanity of her life at that time. I just saw this really calm, cool Aboriginal Grandma who was funny and is really enjoying her life. That's what I saw. That's what I was attracted to. But I could also relate to the story. It was a great example of, no matter how far down the ladder we fall, we can always make it back. And when we do we can make a difference in other people's lives. Absolutely. For sure that's the story.

Meeting all these people, especially in Alberta, they now know Ruth is my adopted Grandma. They'll always come up to me and say,

"Hey, you know Ruth?" I'll go, "Yeah I do." They'll say, she's my cousin, or she's my Grandma, or she's my sister's best friend. It's amazing how many people know Ruth and I'll run into that all over Alberta and even in Ontario; Ruth had been at a conference, and made an impact on somebody, which she usually does. So that's kind of cool to be part of that.

Recently, I saw my little girl, Skylar, getting her name in a ceremony. It was done on a Buffalo hide. Being in that kind of situation and being comfortable with it, that was totally out of character for her, especially being out at Siksika. She's stapled to her Mom, they are very close. She's not used to that, but for her to just get up and be part of the ceremony. But that's Ruth. That's who she is. She just makes everything calm and trusting and she's totally accepting of anything.

Whatever Ruth has to give, she's willing to give it, if you're willing to go on the journey with her. That's what I've experienced. There is no prejudice, there is no selfishness in her whatsoever. For example, the guy that she "named" the other night, he's a white guy. It doesn't matter though. That's what I love about the Aboriginal people. I'm a white guy. I look like a white guy but I'm Metis, I'm blood Indian. But nobody ever once said, you can't be here, you can't be doing this or that. They accepted me instantly because I was interested in that spirituality, that calm, that serenity that everybody looks for. I think these people like me, because I don't care what people think. I care enough about myself to exhaust every option there is to find peace and serenity and happiness in my life, because I know what it was like when I didn't have it. The insanity of that, as opposed to going to a sweat...I think I'll go to a sweat.

If people would just open their eyes. I have seven and a half years of sobriety because I found a higher power of my own understanding. So it's got a little bit of Blackfoot, a little bit of Blood, a little bit of Metis, a little bit of Cree, a little bit of this and that.

I believe we're coming to a place in humanity where we're going to see the end of organized religion because they've done so much damage to people. People are losing faith in organized religion.

I've just found this other way that's just very simple. It's not complicated. When you're nine years old and you go to confession and the priest goes, well, say ten Hail Mary's. What are you talking about? I'm not a sinner, I'm nine years old. It doesn't make any sense to me. And with Aboriginal spirituality it's simple. I get up in the morning and I look outside and every two or three days there's this Eagle that flies around here, and I know I'm doing exactly what I should be doing. It's all I need. It's like a check in. I relate to that. Where am I with my spirituality today? I don't see some guy on a cross or a stake.

I know now that probably the reason I am back here in Calgary, was that Ruth was saying to the Creator, "Make sure you take care of this guy." She told me she always thought something bad was going to happen but I knew she always had my back spiritually – that's for sure. She gets it. So many people out there don't get it. Just the meaning of life. Period. Everybody thinks its rocket science.

With Ruth, she doesn't think about the past or tomorrow, she just thinks about the present, which is really Buddhism. She's figured it out, to be present in the moment. If we take a drink there is none of that. All that ends right then and there. So why wouldn't we enjoy twenty-four hours at a time, which is the one day at a time saying. I think she lives her life by that. She enjoys absolutely every single second of every moment of every day and it's just a repeat, repeat, repeat. She gets up, she prays, she does what she needs to do and then at night she repeats it.

I think the best story is how, after many years of no contact, that she knew that I needed help. She walked through the door of my business. You know, I think I would have continued with long term sobriety, but I don't think I would be the person I am today without her help. She helped me, and in turn I need to help as many people as I can myself, the same way she's done for so many people. The

113

other night at the naming ceremony, one of the guy's that she named. I don't know who he is. But that's Ruth. She has many, many people that she's helped and she doesn't even talk about it. To me that's humility and to me that's another thing that's important because as alcoholics, we have such huge egos. So to get humility and serenity...

I remember I was in Santa Fe back when, just miserable and just basically trying to die somehow, someway. And I remember I used to have a friend in Moose Jaw that I used to golf with in the summer time. He's one of those adventurous guys that takes a month from his family and goes somewhere. And he said he went to Tibet and lived on the side of a mountain with a Buddhist monk for a month. Just sat on the side of this mountain for a month. So I had exhausted every option in my life and I thought, I should just book that thing right now. That's how desperate I was. I didn't want to die, but I didn't know how to live so I was like, I've got to find some kind of sanity or serenity or anything. So it wasn't too long after I tried to kill myself that I started thinking towards that. Sure enough, my boy phoned and I moved back to Calgary.

A year later Grandma Ruth walks in the door. So it's like, what is this all about? I don't have an answer, nor do I want the answer. Just go with it.

Interlude - Jim Pritchard

# back to Omakh

*A friend described these interludes as "search scenes." That made sense, we were searching for places.*

*It was like we were searching for a place that represented time before memory, the sacred relationship between Ruth's people, her ancestors and the land. Was Ruth searching for her own story, putting the pieces together in a narrative with an all encompassing meaning? Were we searching for our relationship, trying to understand it, the relationship between white and red? Searching for the future, and how we get there?*

*We knew we were searching for a circle on a high place- looking for the Medicine Wheel – a piece of a puzzle, in search of a question.*

It was time to make another attempt to find the Majorville Medicine Wheel. It was now October and we wanted to get out before the snow began to fly. This time I actually wanted us to find it. It was cloudy on this Saturday morning and I wondered about the weather. I phoned Ruth to see what she thought. She was pretty clear, telling me that we made a plan, and we needed to carry through with it, so let's go.

Medicine Wheels are significant to Aboriginal people, and the Majorville Wheel is one of the largest and oldest in North America.

It has been researched by the University of Calgary and many others. Evidence suggests it is 5000 years old, as old as the Pyramids. The Blackfoot refer to it as "Omahkiyaahkohtoohp", meaning "old, big arrangement," or "Omahk" for short. The Blackfoot see the Medicine Wheel as being sacred. Elders have referred to it as, "the place where the spirits search."

The Medicine Wheel is located within a lease area. Before I headed out I contacted Darren, the Lease Foreman. Darren was driving around out in the area. He answered his cell phone.

"Hello Darren, my name is Jim Pritchard. Me and a friend are planning to visit the Medicine Wheel today. Just thought I would let you know.

"Okay, what time are you coming?" Darren sounded like a really friendly guy.

"Probably get there around noon" I guessed.

"So what will you be driving?" Darren followed up.

"Oh, a brownish SUV," was my description.

"Well, should be fine. There shouldn't be too many people around out there today, maybe a few hunters," he informed.

"Okay," I acknowledged.

"It has been dry out there all season, no moisture, so I suggest you don't light any fires," was his understatement.

"OK, so how do I get there? We've tried before once," was my key question.

Darren gave me directions. They sounded pretty clear, after all he knows his way around this area.

I thanked him, "Well great, sounds good." And then I added, "Do you mind if I call back later if I need more direction?"

"Not at all", he said. Good, I thought, we might be talking.

I headed out from Calgary and met Ruth at her office at the Elders Lodge at Siksika. As usual she was milling about talking to people who were coming and going, chatting with the residents and visitors. She seemed to know everyone and, as always, she introduced me, this is my friend Jim, this is my cousin, my nephew, my sister in law, my friend. I always enjoy these introductions and meeting these friendly people.

Off we went, heading South across the Bow River and over the flatlands towards Majorville, the land rolling out endlessly under the huge sky. I explained to Ruth the instructions that I had received and, picking up where we had left off last time, that we needed to keep heading east at the Highline, across the Texas gate, and take a right at the fork in the road. With our new directions we passed the stone that Ruth had talked about last time and eventually across the gate. We came to a fork in the road where we headed off to the right and then South for a few miles on a dirt track road. When we came to a rise looking off to the vast South with no sign of hills, I stopped and got out. I looked around and decided to place a call to Darren. Ruth sat in the vehicle, I was hoping she wouldn't light a cigarette.

"Hey Darren, it's Jim again," I hoped I wasn't annoying him.

"Hi," he said warmly.

"We took the fork south, but I can't see anything like a gate and we've come a few miles," my attempt to describe a vast space with no clear markers, like a street sign!

"Well, it sounds like you have taken the wrong turn, and gone off too far," he said helpfully. "Turn around, go back and keep going along the road, until the Highline is on your left. Then look for a sign on a gate. Open and close it, then keep going, you will be close."

"Good, will do. Thanks again Darren."

Feeling like we were never going to reach the Wheel, and that the reference points in this vastness were too vague, we backtracked and followed the directions until, to some relief, we found the gate, opened it, and proceeded through.

From there it was another few miles through what would have been a compact car- devouring road. I said to Ruth, "Well, it's good we're not driving that little car you used to have back in the day."

"Oh, for sure," she agreed. "Oh for sure" is one of Ruth's trademark expressions, a sure sign of agreement, and affirmation. It feels like, "We're good."

"What was that car called?" I asked.

"A Gremlin, I think," she said.

I smiled, "The weird looking one with no back on it."

"The one with no behind. HO!" she explodes, then bursts out in laughter. This is another of Ruth's signature expressions, "HO!" a rare, but remarkable sound, half scream, half exclamation, all joy. You can't help but share in the moment. That sound makes me feel good.

"Oh, we're crazy, you and me." said Ruth.

"HO!" I let out. "Holy," she laughed, covering her mouth with her hand. Priceless, I thought.

We carried on a short distance in my four-wheel drive until a large hill emerged ahead of us. We knew we were there.

The final run-up to the Medicine Wheel leads to a fence around the bottom of the hill. We stopped to have the lunch that I had prepared. We headed up the trail to the top of the hill. It was steep enough, but Ruth is strong and healthy and soon we were on the top. We found ourselves beside a central cairn of stones at the center of 28 spokes of stones, radiating outwards.

Among the stones in the center cairn were various spiritual offerings, crystals, crosses, sweetgrass, various tokens. Ruth offered a prayer, crushing out some tobacco amongst the stones. We were still as she said a prayer, recognizing the spirits.

It occurred to me that, for Ruth, these sites are not archaeological. This is not book history, or museum history. There is a deep sense of identity as a people and place. They are as important today as they were thousands of years ago. All these places, the stones, the effigies, the wheels, are connected continuously through millennia, and inhabited by a people, like a cultural braid. More than a physical place, this site is spiritual, a center of space, of time, the four directions, of all life. As I stood, feeling this space, I heard the echo of Ruth's comment from our last trip, "My ancestors, on my back, I feel them."

We then walked around, quietly talking. We followed a path down the slope facing west, towards a formation of larger rocks towards the bottom. We marvelled at the uniqueness of each stone, covered in mosses, some orange, like each one crafted in the imagination of an artist.

At one point Ruth said that she wanted to smoke. Trying not to be controlling, I said I didn't think that was a good idea, as Darren had cautioned us about the extreme dry conditions. She didn't respond. I felt her smiling. Was she playing with me? Was she just going to go ahead and smoke anyway? I kept my fingers crossed. We climbed back to the top of the hill and wandered a bit more. We scanned hundreds of square miles, hills, coulees, bluffs, small glints of towns in the distance.

Then Ruth felt it was time to head down as it was getting cold and windy. She left, heading back down. I would catch up. I watched as she became smaller against the immense background. I sensed her oneness with it all, a peacefulness.

After we got back in the car, we went down for a look at the Bow River, rippling through its deep carve in the prairie. We never saw another person the whole time we were out there.

We were satisfied that we had found the Medicine Wheel this time and agreed we could look forward to visiting again. This is surely an important place to Ruth and her People. It is a solid reminder of the long history of this People on this Land. I decided to place a quick call to Darren. "Darren, Jim here, just wanted to let you know we found the place. Hey, thanks for your help"

"Oh great, glad you made it. You're welcome," I never met Darren, but I think I would like him.

Heading back across the landscape, I asked Ruth, "Hey, did you ever have that smoke?"

"No, I didn't think it was a good idea, too dry," she responded.

Why was I worried? I asked myself.

It seemed important for us to come here and connect with this ancient site, something that Ruth really wanted to revisit, and for me to see, part of the process of sharing the history of her People.

"Well, a good day," I said satisfied, "I'm glad we found it this time."

Looking off as we passed the stone we had stopped on our last trip, Ruth agreed, "Oh for sure."

# Part V

# Leadership and Healing

"Let's heal our People, let's get our People well."

## Chapter 9 speaking for the People

*Beginning in 1993, Ruth spent 18 years as an elected member of the Siksika Band Council. A year before that she ran as a candidate for the Provincial Government riding, largely non-Aboriginal, that includes her Nation.*

It goes way back. In my heart, I always wanted to be in the political arena, where I could have some impact, maybe make some change for our People. I wanted to be a voice, not just for Natives, but for all people, particularly minorities. Women, especially, have little voice. They need an advocate to be heard, and move toward equality. We have to recognize that women are often the backbone of our communities, the ones who get things done. So, to find that voice was the important thing. My mouth had been shut for so many years. For Aboriginal people in general, there have been few choices. The Indian Agent, the Priests, the Government, they made the choices for us.

It is our responsibility as Elders to show the way for our youth. Also, especially for our young women, to show an example of how to be assertive, to speak up, that they are as good as anyone. As a child, I was prepared for this by being introduced by my Father to the traditional ways. Other Elders also opened my eyes. There was Mary White Elk, who had a little education, who wasn't afraid to challenge the Indian Agent. She was one of the first female leaders, here at Siksika. Then there was Lila Healy, my cousin. These were female role models. I try to follow in their footsteps, to not take second place, to speak up about the problems and issues we face.

My first experience was in March 1992, when I ran for the New Democratic Party. Bob Hawkesworth talked to me about running. It was a bi-election in the Provincial riding of Little Bow, which ran all the way from Siksika almost down to Lethbridge, a huge area that included our Nation. So I thought, we'll give it a try. But I ran into a lot of racism and prejudice, especially down in rural areas south of Siksika.

I still have those clippings at home, the things they said about me in the paper. The Lethbridge headline was "Gleichen Granny ND Candidate." It was sort of, look at this old Native granny, she wants to run for public office. Other comments that were made were like, "Who the hell do you think you are to be running for public office?"
Those kind of things I experience, they just make me stronger. When these things happen, they hurt my feelings, of course they hurt. But I have that resilience. I would just bounce back. I don't take on that garbage. It just helps me to work more and it helps me to be stronger, and reinforces for me that I am here to help people. I'm here for a purpose. I got my shots in too. I told a reporter that even if the Alberta Government didn't officially support two languages, I would... English and Blackfoot, because Blackfoot, our language, is the second most common in the riding, and I speak both! The main thing is, I wanted to show that there are a lot of ordinary people who have been ignored and left out.

During my campaign Elijah Harper came out to support me. He was an ND from Manitoba, the first Treaty Indian to be elected there as a Provincial politician. He was famous for standing up for Aboriginal recognition in Canada. He was gentle and soft spoken. We had a Round Dance and a feast for him. He passed away in 2013, and I don't think it got a lot of recognition in the media, for all the work he had done for Aboriginal people, his commitment.

I worked hard. I won over ten per cent of the vote, and came in third, ahead of the Social Credit and the Alliance. I always thought that I could help out. There are lots of political issues that we face as Native people, like poverty, education, and addictions.

When I was at home at Siksika in 1993, the Native Women's Shelter opened in Calgary. It took time for the people to get to know me because I was away for 35 years. I had to really get to know the people of Siksika. This happened through all the training and all the healing that I helped with at Siksika.

Then people started to ask me to run for Band Council in the Fall of 1993 – some were Elders, some of them were women in my training sessions. They felt that I would be a really good candidate, to get nominated, to get elected, to speak on their behalf. It took time for me to really think about it. I was doing a lot of work at home to help our People deal with a lot of their issues. I always felt, maybe I should take another step to really help out people. So I listened to the Elders when they asked me to run. The late Russell Wright and my late cousin Julia Wright, they asked me to run. My late great aunt, Mrs. Bad Boy, the one that gave me the name Awo Taanaakii was always asking me. I talked to my family, whoever I felt it was important to get that approval and their support. They felt I should just run.

This was another challenge I had to take in my life. Before I made that decision I was thinking back to my late uncle, Alex Scalp Lock. He told me he saw me in a vision where I would be with the Chief and Council at Siksika one day. He told me that I had to really speak for our People, speak on their behalf.

Alex had told me, "Look, Niitkanii, my little sister, there's a road that you're on, you've been walking on this road and one day you're going to be ready. You just continue walking. There's always jealousy, there's always bad talk. Don't listen to those negative things, just keep walking, put your head up and make sure you have that vision, and you're going to reach whatever your vision is."

I was really thinking about it, well maybe this is the time. When you're in your healing process there's always that "spirit time," when you really know and feel deep down you're ready, and I was thinking, well, I've got all these people supporting me, Elders especially, and the women too. Those things really stayed with me.

I ran and I was elected.

My Grandmother was still alive, Margaret Bad Boy. After I got elected and was going to these pow wows back home, she said, "I don't like it, you wear your high heels and then a shawl, that's not traditional," and she said, "I'm going to help you with that. You always have to look at the traditional way of being a leader. It's okay to wear your high heels to meetings, but you're a traditional leader now, that's how they look at our leaders, you have to honour our tradition."

My late cousin Julia Wright designed the outfit. Our Grandma paid for the buckskin material, even the labour. That's how I got my buckskin dress and my moccasins. So at the inauguration of the Council, I had my buckskin outfit. I was so proud.

I wear that outfit at special meetings, also when we had our 125th anniversary of Treaty 7, when Ralph Klein was out at Siksika. Sometimes I wear it at the grand entry of the pow wow, occasions like that. I have put it away with all those things my Grandma prepared me, including the tipi. She said she wanted to make sure I had these things in my home, for myself, my husband, my children, my grandchildren.

So all those years I was on Council, my Grandma was my biggest support. She stood behind me and she told me, "When you have those meetings, don't just sit there looking pretty. You're going to have to learn to speak up about anything that you disagree with. Raise your hand and say your piece." She prepared me. Her late husband Dick Bad Boy was a member of Council many years ago. She knew.

She always told me she was praying for me for the strength to continue what I'm doing. She always liked it when I went to visit her. If I'm having a hard time I would go see her, for prayers. I was still on Council when we celebrated her 100 year birthday. She knew we were going to have this birthday for her and right away she told the family, I'm going to get Awo Taanaakii to tell the story of my 100 years. I still have that paper, all the things that she experienced in those 100 years. I had to do some research with the Elders. Some of her language was the old Blackfoot – I couldn't really understand. But, for me, of all her grandchildren, to tell the other children in the family, well I'm going to get Awo Taanaakii to tell my life story - it made me feel so special.

The important thing that I wanted to achieve was for Siksika to be a healthy nation. What I mean is to speak out for, I don't like to use the term "the less fortunate," but meaning people who are still struggling with alcohol, and to help them to be able to get on with our lives.

I was involved in many initiatives, anything to do with social issues. I really pushed for ways to deal with our social problems, anything to do with social programs, to be a spokesperson or to be part of a negotiating team. The Chief was always appointing me to be part of this team because they know how I negotiate, how I speak to the issue as it pertains to Siksika people.

We negotiated with the Province to help us with some funding for a place for people in crisis. Since we got our liquor rights in Alberta, so many of our people were hit on the railroad track while consuming alcohol in the town of Gleichen. These are the kind of tragic things that happened after we got our "liquor rights" in the mid 1960's. I was part of that team and we met with Dr. Lyle Oberg, the MLA for our area. We negotiated, and I was so happy when we got this Crisis Centre going, because I felt that we're always in this crisis mode. It's about time we had a place to go when someone dies from alcohol or anything relating to alcohol, or domestic violence, or car accidents. We never, back home at that time, had a place for our people to go. The Crisis Centre is still going on the Nation.

Elected to Council, when I speak, I always speak my truth. On the day I was inaugurated I swore on the Bible, and I swore on the Siksika logo, and the peace pipe, that I'm going to serve Siksika to the best of my ability. That means being sober. Being raised traditional I look at my role as a leader, not just a job and a paycheck, but to help our people. I always look at my purpose, what I swore on, and our code of ethics for Council. I can't even say I missed five or six days of work in eighteen years. My whole heart was into the commitment.

I spent endless hours going to meetings. My husband, Francis Melting Tallow, would drive me to Edmonton, sometimes to Vancouver, sometimes to Winnipeg. We even went on a trip to Toronto. I give a lot of thanks to my husband because he supported me right through.

There was a lot of bad talk in the community. I experienced verbal put downs by some of the men in the community, behind my back or on paper. They talked personal stuff, like, I always have long fingernails, or my hair, and one time I was told I had a face lift!

At times when I spoke in chambers, there was some kind of rebuttal or smart remark. For example, the Sundance Arbor was named Gordon Yellow Fly Arbor, so I was giving Council some history to do with Gordon Yellow Fly, who died in the Second World War and was buried overseas. This building was named after him. I always feel that the younger Council members needed to get some history of these things. We don't just name a building any name. People would roll their eyes and say, oh here she goes again, telling these old stories. There's always history, there's pride, because this man served in the war. He died for us to have this freedom. So I said, well, how many of you have family or relatives that will tell you about some of the history? I was very fortunate to grow up in that era. I listened to what's important. One day I'd like to share it with our young people.

My name, Shield Woman, the shield is a protection for me. Little do these people know its sacred meaning. The sacred meaning is a protection for me and also the Shelter. So no matter what people do to try and hurt me, it just bounces back. The shield protects others, my family, my friends, and the abused women, men – because now I work with the men too– and many people. But not once did I retaliate. I don't believe in retaliation or revenge. I always look at what I believe, because I really believe in Jesus, in the Creator. I felt I had a purpose, to help people at all levels. I look on the positive of why people elected me. That's why I was on council for eighteen years, because many of them believed me. These little put downs, these petty things, they don't mean anything to me.

It is unfortunate, but it is because of our history. It has been passed on from our experience, the residential schools. They call it lateral violence, when you act like you have been treated. It happens all over the Native communities. There is a lot of jealousy, bullying, and abuse. We act out what we have learned, and it continues generation after generation. We cover the pain with alcohol and prescription drugs. It keeps coming up as forms of violent behaviour. This is why we need to focus on our healing, so we can support each other. I can understand politics, but when people get personal, like talking about how you look, I think that's personal. That's what I mean, our people need a lot of healing.

Leadership means to lead people, to lead men, women, children, the community. I was told a story by one of the Elders about a man who was drinking, running around, and he was ousted out of Council. They took away his Council medal. They took away his medal – they got rid of him – because they were so strict back in the past. You couldn't carry on drinking, or run around. I always look at those traditional ways of being an Elder, a leader. A Blackfoot Siksika leader should be free from alcohol, should be free from drugs, should have a healthy lifestyle, should speak the language, should have education to some degree, and have balance.

I believe you should look at the Reserve globally, never favour anyone. If my family approached me I would send them to somebody else. I always focused on the big picture of Siksika. I was the oldest of the Chief and Council in my last term and I always felt, well, I'm here for a purpose. I always had my inauguration oath on my desk, a reminder to me every day I'm sitting in the chambers. It's not about me.

I did so much healing over the years, on my sobriety. I'd get up in the morning with a clear mind and I'd pray first thing in the morning for that day to be a good day. If I felt offended I dealt with it, sometimes right then and there, or I excused myself from the Chambers, in order for me to have clarity.

People need somebody to go talk to, somebody that will listen. I'd communicate with the Elders in Blackfoot, because they always feel so much better when we spoke in our language. A leader should be friendly. You go out and talk to people. My husband knows I like to visit, I like to talk to people – maybe somebody's having a hard time, a bad day – I take time for that person, regardless of who they are. When I was on Council people would phone me, there were a few times other members would cuss and swear at me over the phone. I would listen to them, let them vent. Then I would tell them, why don't you come in, we'll sit down and have a meeting. I'll spend some time with you. But none of them showed up. They know they could tell me anything, and I'm not going to sit there getting defensive or start behaving the way they are. You should be a good person to talk to, and in our traditional meaning for a leader, the head Chief of the reserve is the Grandfather and the Council members are the parents.

Once I was told by an Elder, "When people are jealous, when they talk like that to you, they want to change their lives, they don't want to be you, but they see the good things about a person that's healthy and they want to get there."

When I was on Council, one of the Elders, Russell Wright, said I was his Mother. I said, "Oh my gosh, you're way older than me, how could I be your mother?" I kind of gave him a strange look, and he looked at me and in Blackfoot he said, "Tell me why you're reacting that way?" and I told him, "You're a respected Elder Russell, and I just got newly elected into Council, and I'm way younger than you, how could I be your Mother?" So he started telling me, "In the Blackfoot culture, when you're on Council, you're a parent, the Chief is the Grandfather, the members of Council are the parents." It had to take an Elder to explain it to me, that I was a Mother to all the people in Siksika.

There was this friend of mine, passed away now, that I went to residential school with. She used to always come in and I was already on Council and she'd be crying to me. She was a battered woman, she had a drinking problem and she said, "Ruth I just cannot get going with my life and I want to be like you." I told her, "You can't be me, you are you. You could change, you could do some healing, you could sober up."

I believe in people. Working with so many people throughout the years, people do change. I have faith in people, I have hope in people. There's a time when we're ready, according to spirit's time, and that's when we make those changes, with the support in place.

I've always felt we should have put more focus on helping our people to deal with their alcohol problems, their domestic issues and with education. Let's heal our people, let's get our people well, before we build big fancy buildings. Those could come in time, but I always believed, with what we've gone through, traumatized all these years and blaming everybody else, that we have to work on that first. It's a responsibility on individuals, but we could be innovative, we could create more programs or ways to help our people, especially our young people.

I always say, whatever we're doing, in education, in programs, there always has to be a component to do with our way, the Blackfoot traditional way. That's why the Shelter was built, our Native

Women's Shelter. We should have our Indian way, like parenting, teaching our young people, even to do with the treaties, the historical causes. A lot of young people don't know, even the older generation don't always know, because a lot of them grew up in the residential school. They didn't know a lot of these things. I always say I'm so fortunate. I went to those ceremonies and listened to all those Elders. Little did I know at that time that all that stuff would be helping me today.

A great highlight for me was when I was supported by Band Council and I was nominated for an Esquao Award in 2000 in Edmonton. It is an Award sponsored by the Institute for the Advancement of Aboriginal Women. Esquao is a Cree word meaning woman. It was important to me because it was a Lifetime Achievement Award.

Eventually, I didn't get re-elected. My heart wasn't in it anymore. After 18 years I really missed that human contact, one to one with people. I'm so happy in the kind of work that I'm doing today, working with these abused victims, even the men. I'm really making headway with the men. I couldn't really do all that work when I was on Council. Right now, I'd rather help somebody on an individual basis.

I'm really happy I was on Council. Some of the terminology I didn't really understand, like when we dealt with the Government, but I always asked, I'd say, "I didn't understand what you said," or I raised my hand, "Okay, can you repeat what you're saying?" to make sure I understand. I'm not a highly educated woman. But in 2013 I completed my Certificate at the Banff Center, Aboriginal Leadership and Management Excellence. Leroy Wolf Collar, a former Chief, made sure he sent us to the school in Banff to get these negotiating skills, and all these courses.

Things happen when it's the right time and that's Spirit time. I had fulfilled my purpose as a leader, to do it in a traditional way. Now it was time to move on, and keep supporting the healing of our Nation.

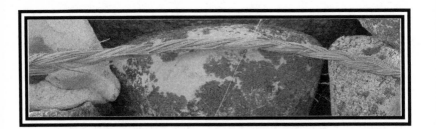

## Chapter 10 healing, to see the beauty

I was in attendance in Ottawa a few years ago when the Prime Minister apologized to the Native people. It was June 12, 2008. I was sent as the representative of the Siksika Chief and Council as the oldest member. I was also a survivor of the residential schools.

I went on a late flight and I went to the meeting. I had a hard time finding a place to sit because it is the House of Commons, where they have people sitting up high and then down low, all around.

To me, it didn't feel genuine from the Prime Minister. I think he was just going through the motions. Maybe his intentions were good, but I didn't feel it was genuine. I just started crying. I think it had a lot to do with my own stuff, and part of it came from him. I didn't feel that he knew just exactly where we were coming from, and how it has impacted the people all these years, generation after generation. Maybe ignorance on his part, I don't know. Maybe he didn't really do some homework on the whole thing to do with residential schools. I'm not putting this guy down. It's just how I was feeling at the time. I couldn't stop crying. I saw so many people there, women, men, young people, and there was so much crying there. Maybe I was especially feeling for the Elders who were there – some were crippled up, I won't say from the drinking, but something must have happened to them, some tragedies. I really felt that pain. It was so heavy.

I really felt for the Elders, for their pain. I had time to talk to them and it was more like a healing for me, to be there, to witness it and experience it personally. It was good in the long run that the apology took place, and that I was there to experience it. I came to terms with it. I don't go on thinking, no it wasn't genuine, but at the time that's how I felt. It was a long time coming. I always say society should be educated on how we've been traumatized, right from day one – society needs to know why it's like it is today for us.

It's been from one generation to the next and I always feel, especially in my healing work, that there's a responsibility that we have – we cannot stay stuck. With the kind of work that I do, I teach people to take onus, to say, "Okay, this is what happened to me." We have so many resources today and it is a time for us to heal. We cannot stay stuck. It's an individual thing, when you've been abused and traumatized. We have to take on this responsibility and say, "Okay, I'm an alcoholic" and this and that. Of course, I feel the pain for these people. But with the help of Elders and these different resources, I always feel that it's time for us to move on, instead of stuck in it- in that black hole.

For me healing looks at the whole, the four aspects of yourself, the Medicine Wheel. You look at the emotional, you look at the spiritual, you look at the physical, the mental. These are all the parts of our whole self. We have to look at all of these four parts for wellness, how our body is, how we feel, how we think. For me, when working with people, I always look at building that foundation – the spiritual part. I'm not connected to a religious group or anything like that. Once you've been abused, once someone invades your space, you lose that spirit. You end up running around, maybe drinking, or abusive. But once the Holy Spirit comes back, you let go of all the stuff that happened to you. I talk through experience, because when I was drinking I was like a zombie, running around. I lost my spirit and it took me a long time to come to terms with asking the Spirit to come back into my heart, and let him take control of my life. I feel so much better today.

My Blackfoot name, Awo Taanaakii – it's a very spiritual name.

When I'm going to pray I always ask, Awo Taanaakii, Awo Taanaakii, Awo Taanaakii, at least three times. That's when I make the connection and I find that it's easy for me to pray then, so simple when I make that connection. In the morning, I feel so much better and acknowledge that there's a being higher or more powerful than me. If I don't pray, my day doesn't go right.

I never ask for money or things, but for a good day. I thank the Creator, the Holy Spirit, that I'm awake and sober. It's been a long road, 40 years sobriety. I'm so thankful. I have gratitude. The things I did to my body, my mind, when I was drinking-it took me a long time in my journey to look at what I did to myself by drinking that alcohol. For me today to be sober – there's always reminders of how important it is to me when I see people, not just here at Siksika, but anywhere who are caught up in drinking.

One time, long ago, I was in a complete blackout. I was drinking downtown- skid row. Oh, it's such a scary experience. I woke up at a playground, I think Centre Street North in Calgary. It was in the summer time. I was just hanging onto a brown bag – I had a bottle of wine in there. I woke up and I was shivering. I sat up and I was thinking, oh my gosh, where am I, how in the world did I get here? And I was sitting on the bench and right away I took a big snort out of the wine and I put it back inside my jacket – of course I got feeling good again and I went home. My kids weren't with me at that time. They were living down in Saskatchewan with their Grandmother. I went home and there was nobody. You know these are some of the experiences – being in a blackout-anything could have happened to me. I never found out how in the world I got up there, but for me to wake up in a playground...

I'm not a registered psychologist or whatever. I have experience, I worked in halfway houses in Calgary, alcohol treatment, the women's shelter. What I do is I like to sit down with people, man or woman – and the color of your skin to me doesn't mean anything – talk to an individual and ask the person, "How can I help?" I always tell them, "I'm here to help you and I can only share my experience with you." I always tell them I understand where they are coming from – I never make any kind of judgment. I explain what alcohol does to an individual, psychologically, physically, and that it's a disease. When I was drinking, most of the time I didn't eat, so my body was always craving for that sugar. When I quit drinking 40 years ago, I was diagnosed with liver damage, so I really did a number to my liver and my brain. All that happened because I drank wine. If I had a few dollars, maybe I would have a shot of vodka or whiskey or beer. These are some of the things I share with individuals. If they tell me they have a drinking problem, I always tell them I can help them with that, especially the spiritual part. It's so important to start making that connection. The way it is, that process, it's so simple to make that connection. Once the spirit is home, back in your heart, then you make that connection.

When I work with people, there's different questions I ask them. I don't talk about religious beliefs and all these manmade judgments. One of the things I ask them is, do you pray, somehow? Like my Father used to tell me, regardless of what kind of background we come from, the Creator or Jesus, whatever term we have for this higher power, he will listen to you. It's so true, because regardless of how low I went, it was always in the back of my mind, one day my life would change.

I burn sweet grass with people sometimes, and if I feel I need extra help, I ask an Elder to come in with me. I sense the feelings in that healing circle, because sometimes they can be very heavy. There's so much pain in there. One of the things I really stress is forgiveness – you have to forgive yourself first before you can forgive somebody else. Ask the Creator to help you to forgive.

You can tell how healed people are, any people. Some are angry, they carry that around. They put blame on others, nothing is their fault. You can see how they walk around, like they have a barrier up, an attitude like they are not approachable. Healing takes a lot of work, soul-searching: why am I angry? You have to become aware of yourself. You can also tell a person who is on a healing journey. They walk taller. They are happier and open to people, simple little things, like say, "Good morning" to people.

I always take time for people, regardless how long this person takes to disclose. I always talk about confidentiality – whatever we share in here, stays in here. Sometimes I give them a piece of paper to write down what they want to talk about. Let's say, this is just an example, I experienced abuse from one of my siblings - they would write it down. Once they read this paper, what they're going to talk about or deal with, after everybody has a chance to talk about what they wrote down, I ask them to put these pieces of paper in the center. There's sweet grass or fire, they throw them in there, so everything that they shared in that room, it's dealt with and it's gone. I participate too – I still have some pain in me that I still deal with. Healing is a lifetime thing and it's every day for me. This is how I look at it. Even now thinking about it, I still get emotional because there's still a lot of garbage that I have to deal with. I could never say I'm totally healed.

Today, I look at my self. I don't drink anymore. I have that freedom. When things don't go good for me, I don't run to alcohol. I look at the consequences of what happened to me when I was running to alcohol. I can really understand the people that I work with, because it's scary when you throw in the towel, the first time when you say, "okay, today's the day." Especially when you look around – people who don't have family, don't have children, don't have Elders. At least with drinking, you know you don't have to deal with it. You can run to the bottle. I didn't have to face the consequences and I kept running away from myself. It's scary, everything, the pain, the bottle, the blackouts, and even leaving it.

Some people don't believe that I'm a recovering alcoholic. They look at me as this woman who's never had problems. But I always tell them, especially if they're older, I tell them, "well thank God you didn't see me." I didn't do most of my drinking here at Siksika. I did most of my drinking in Calgary, Red Deer, Thompson, Winnipeg, Regina, because I kept running. It caught up to me and I could no longer run.

I was the worst thief.  I was the worst liar. I even lied to a priest in Calgary, a good priest. He was one of the Principals at the School. He was in Calgary when I was drinking back in 1973 and he was really good to me. I phoned him up one day. I was so sick, along with my cousin and some other women. We were so sick, we had nothing else to drink.

I phoned up Father and asked him, "Father, I'm really sick.  I've got this prescription from my doctor that I have to have Brandy." He believed my story. "Okay," he says, "I'll come over. I'll come pick you up." And my three other friends they came with us to the liquor store up on 16$^{th}$ avenue by the Beacon Hotel.  Father gave me this 20 dollar bill, and said, "Okay, I'll wait for you, I'll take you girls back home, because I don't want you drinking around." He knew I was drinking all that Spring and Summer. I didn't even get brandy. I got a half a gallon of wine. I got back into the car and he looked in there and he said, "Oh Rute!" because he couldn't pronounce Ruth, he used to say Rute, really hard. He said," Rute, you remind me of the Devil's Sister!" Of course, I just laughed it off.

———————————

The first step in the Residential School settlement process was the common experience claim, for anyone who had been in the schools. So I applied for that. That was fairly straightforward, I needed to document all the years I had been in the school. I got my settlement. When I got the check, it was deposited into my account. The day I went to the bank machine, well I didn't expect it that day. Oh my gosh, I just about dropped. I was just standing there, I couldn't believe it, the receipt that comes out. But I was so upset. I was so close to swearing. Honest, this money I got, it's supposed to help me? I was just standing there, then I left, I just started crying. I couldn't even take any of the money out.

The second step is an application for compensation for individual acts of sexual or physical abuse at the school. You have to be really prepared to give the specifics of what happened to you. I had a real good lawyer, a Native lawyer. I went for my hearing under the Residential School Settlement Process, out at Siksika. There was me, my lawyer, an adjudicator, and a couple of other people representing the Government of Canada.

The hearing lasted all day. I felt like running out of that room and I cried most of the interview. The abuse claim interview, holy, I was so angry. My lawyer would look at me, and he knew that there was some stuff that I was being asked, he knew some of the time I couldn't handle it. He would call for a break. There were even times, my lawyer, he had tears in his eyes. He was affected. He would ask for a break. I would go out, start crying. I don't know how long it lasted. They were asking the difficult questions about the abuse, the times, the details. How can a young child at that time remember, the times when it happened, what time of the day, the week? How am I supposed to remember all that? It's strange, it is hard to remember details from sixty years ago. Yet, it is always there, it comes back and I think about it, see it, all the time. It never goes away, just keeps surfacing. It was like it happened yesterday.

On my application, I put on there, I may have gone on to university, got a degree, but all the stuff that was happening to me, and the drinking, and I never felt good about myself. I always felt like I was a, I hate to use the word, but a rundown woman who was good for nothing. I was always told I was good for nothing. It took me a long time, especially when I started to sober up, to feel good about myself. After you've been abused, sexual abuse, you feel dirty all the time. All the stuff that was being asked in that interview, I had such a hard time.

After the hearing, I think it took at least six weeks to be myself again. I couldn't even have supper that night. My husband took me for a long drive and all I could drink was water and 7-up. I couldn't keep anything down. Each time I was thinking about the questions, I just got sick to my stomach. I had a lot of help, therapy and counselling. I was so angry. Look at what they took away from me. I was a young person. I could have went on to get a formal education. But look what I had to go through, and all my brothers and sisters.

When my lawyer called me I was in Calgary and he said he had this check. I said, what check? He started laughing. "Oh Ruth, you're expecting this check. Aren't you excited?" I said, "No." After he said, "Well, I don't blame you, but I've got it." He brought it down to Siksika and he bought me this great big basket of things. This was December a few years ago. I told my lawyer, well, thank you very much, because he's so thoughtful. Everything was in there, even a Bible. I still have that Bible, and there was other stuff, all kinds of tea, coffee, everything. I think I enjoyed that basket more than that check because I knew this basket was from him, more on a personal side. I just grabbed that check from him and he looked at me. He said to me, "Ruth, you must still be angry," and I said, "Yes of course, I'm not going to lie." Then he sat down, he had this paper. Once I accepted this check, this payment, I could never go back and make another claim. I told him, it's nothing personal on him. "This check," I couldn't stop saying, "this check." I just grabbed it. I put it in my purse.

Maybe it was ironic there was a Bible in the basket. Maybe he was thinking, in a way, that was for forgiveness. I always say to people I work with, forgiveness is so important. How can you move on if you don't forgive people that hurt you? I guess if I wasn't in my healing, maybe I would have thrown the Bible at him. But I took it in a forgiving way.

Who am I to hang onto these things that happened to me? I came to terms with it. I've forgiven whatever happened to me. I have this freedom. I'm so thankful to be here. I don't blame anybody, I don't blame the government. I don't blame the Priests and Nuns. I feel so much better today. If I don't forgive, it's just hurting myself, me. I don't want that garbage in my life, not to forgive, to be resentful, to have that hate or to dislike. I did a lot of healing and I had to forgive them. If I had a key, forgiveness is the key to healing. If I was still angry, if I didn't forgive, you wouldn't want to be around me. Sure,

I've been sober all these years, but if I hadn't forgiven anybody, I wouldn't be like this today. I would be angry or trying to get back at somebody.

I'm so happy, I move forward. Sometimes I think maybe these things had to happen to me in order for me to do something about my life. That's how I feel and if I didn't experience all that negativity, where would I be today? For me these things were meant to happen, that I didn't get everything on a silver platter. I really had to work hard to get to be where I am today, and to keep helping people, especially at Siksika where I am now. I have been married now for six years to Francis Melting Tallow.

Where will I go from this world? After I go from this life, I know where I'm going. Not to Hell! I'm going to the happy hunting ground in heaven, to be with the angels, to be with Jesus. I believe in Jesus, don't get me wrong. Holy Spirit is going to get me there, because it is here, in my heart, and that's where I'm going to see all my loved ones. To me, there's no such thing as Hell. For us, I know it's just one spirit world.

If I were to die today, I'm ready to go and to see all the people that left me. To see the beauty. I think over the years since I started my sobriety, all the forgiveness, all the people I hurt, all the healing - if I were to die today, I know where I'm going to go. I think I've paid my dues here, I suffered, and I paid back. I try to help people. Since my own hearing, I have provided support to two other people at their hearings. That's so important for people going through this process, which is the hardest thing. I try to treat people with dignity and respect. I don't lie. I don't steal to get ahead. I like to live in a simple way, because I did all those crazy things a long time ago. I'm not saying I'm perfect, I still have a lot of faults.

I always believe in healing. We stumble, we fall flat on our face but when there's somebody holding you by the hand to pick you up and walk with you...we need to live together.

# Sharing Their Stories

The following graciously shared their reflections with Jim

Leroy Wolf Collar

Laura and Olivia

**"a big heart, but a fierce warrior."**

# shared stories: **Leroy Wolf Collar**

*Leroy Wolf Collar is a former Chief of the Siksika Nation. He served on Band Council with Ruth for many years, from 1993-2010, a time when Ruth was firmly back at Siksika, reconnecting* with her community, and developing her community profile as a leader. Leroy is currently completing a degree at the University of Lethbridge.

*We began talking about Leroy's enthusiasm for hockey at Siksika, and his educational career. When we moved the focus to his experiences with Ruth, his intent was clear and easy flowing. He describes Ruth's unique leadership style which combines traditional and contemporary approaches. He clearly illuminates her priority, the welfare of the people, sometimes needing to be fierce in her focus.*

*"Who does that?" reflecting on Ruth's tendency to do anything for people, without thought as to her own convenience or even safety. Then, casting her voice, he says in Blackfoot, "Matapaiya," followed by a pause to make sure I knew what this meant... "they're human."*

---

Working together with Ruth on Siksika Band Council, our first term was the fall of 1993. There were five of us new members that they called rookies at the time. I've always known Ruth as a member of the community, but we weren't close until then. I served six terms in twelve years, and one term as Chief. So I worked with Ruth for fifteen years.

I think it's safe to say we had no political experience and we walked into a time when self-government was being negotiated under the leadership of Chief Strater Crowfoot. So we walked into it unknown, so that was a bit overwhelming for us. In one of the first community meetings, you had the local opposition to self-government negotiations sort of clubbing us over the head - "Who are you guys? Do you know what you're getting yourself into? You're selling the Nation short," and everything about Treaty and Aboriginal rights.

In hindsight we can laugh about it. We got thrown into the water and we had to learn to swim real fast in a shark infested lake. So that was sort of the introduction to politics for us, but you learn fast. It sort of changed our way of thinking because, prior to getting on Council everybody makes certain assumptions to say, well if I get on Council you know I'm going to make sure everybody gets a job, and everybody gets a house, and education is paid for, and we're going to clean up the community... easier said than done.

Ruth, as I know her today, she's a caregiving type person. Her sobriety really emanates her behaviour and her attitude about life. She sort of walks the talk, to say, I've been there, I've been down in the dumps, I know what it's like to get on my feet and I want to make a difference in my life. So, I suppose from her personal experiences, and being who she is today, with so many years of sobriety and having been in her early years a practising alcoholic, as she puts it, she knows what it takes to turn your life around.
Now that she's at the leadership level, she wants to add value to her idea of helping people get on their feet.

We've sat in Council at quiet time when she would share her life experiences, with big dreams and aspirations, what we need in our community's infrastructure to help people get out of their ruts, whether its alcohol or family violence. I know family violence and sobriety is a big issue for her, and she wanted to make that difference at the top.

I remember one time, people had a concern about the practising alcoholics, or whichever way you want to put it, saying, we've got to get rid of those derelicts that keep harassing us every time we come into the Band Office, so somebody needs to get security in, I'm tired of seeing those guys. Ruth was really upset, she blew up and said, "Don't you ever talk that way about those people, they're human beings, they're homeless, they got no jobs, they don't have families and even when they do, they're in the same predicament. How can you say that about those people? How would you like to be in their shoes?"

Ruth was instrumental in helping us to see things from a different perspective. While we're thinking strategic planning, she's thinking survival for those people, saying, they need something to eat, they need a place to sleep and we need to help them. Some of the projects that are here today, the health and wellness centre, she's been instrumental in making that a reality. And of course she pushed for a women's shelter here. I know her preference was, we have to look after our women, why only a men's lodge, why not a women's lodge? She had her moments where she'd be frustrated, to say, these are the perpetrators of family violence, how come we're not accommodating our women who are the victims and survivors of family violence? She helped us to see things.

Ruth is also a very stylish type woman, she takes care of herself, she likes to dress up, she likes to look good, her nails, her hairdos, and her high heels. I always teased her, "Oh Ruth, your fingernails remind me of the Witches of Eastwick!" We have lots of good laughs along our journey.

She's down to earth, non-confrontational. She's real. They don't get any closer to authenticity in living. She's one who often talks about alcohol and drug abuse, not to mention Residential School. I think sometimes she cared too much. She had people that didn't care for her, because she did too much. People are funny that way, there's a sense of jealousy in the community where it's one of those, "Oh she thinks she's too good." We talk about it. There's a division in our community and some of our people don't like to see people succeed, one of those crab theories, when someone's trying to get out and move on, and people are pulling them back down.

As a Councillor, she spoke her mind and she was well versed in the literature that we brought forward as part of the agenda. She's a smart lady. She's got a lot of wisdom and knowledge. As a former Chief, one of the things I wanted for my Councillors was to build capacity in their leadership, management, and governance knowledge. I had them all attend the Banff centre and make sure they all graduated from the Aboriginal Leadership program. So that helped them. She understands what self-government means, what sovereignty means and what the Indian Act is doing to us, very knowledgeable both from the traditional perspective as well as the modern perspective, in leadership and management.

She always raised her issues, whether she was in support or against. Due diligence was a big thing for her, accountability and transparency. If she felt managers or any members of the leadership were not practising healthy lifestyles, she'll speak her mind to Council, to say, I want to bring this issue up here. She says, we're leaders, we're role models, we have to lead by example. Her message is, if we can't do that in our personal lives, we should do the honourable thing and step down. It's bad enough for the victims and survivors of that kind of environment, where alcohol and family violence are the root causes setting us back. People would just go quiet. And then the Chief would say, we'll talk about it some more. She's always pushing for retreats, for healing, we need to talk at our workshops because it's all about healing, we need to heal as leaders in order to walk the talk.

She was just what you would expect in an elected official, addressing issues when they need to be, but following proper protocols and making sure that we're meeting our objectives. When I was Chief she was part of the Human Services team, they were doing the social components, the employment strategies, so she put a lot of emphasis on making those things happen, saying our people needs jobs, and homes.

Ruth spoke her mind, and sometimes, not intentionally stepping on anybody's toes, but she pushed a few buttons when she brought up those issues, and there's people in the room thinking, what is she talking about, get her out of here, that type of thing. They don't say it in those words, but they're not comfortable when she starts talking about healing and getting honest with yourself. There were times when they'd say, oh there she goes again. But she was being honest and she always was pushing the whole idea around that. Most people, Chief Strater Crowfoot, and some of our other colleagues, they were very supportive of her. Everybody for the most part has always been very respectful of her because she took on a lot of issues around healing.

I just became accustomed to her demeanour, and her involvement with off reserve and on-reserve organizations. Even when she ran for the New Democratic Party, I don't think there's anybody brave enough as her to do something like that. It wasn't about who was the most educated among the candidates, it was about the issues. Her underlying objective was, if I can get in as an NDP here, I want the government to understand Aboriginal issues, and that was her main objective. So my hat's off to her.

Ruth had a mother-daughter relationship with Margaret Bad Boy. In Indian country, everybody adopts each other in a traditional way. If we had to do a genealogical tree, it would be difficult for anybody to put that together. I lived with the old lady way back before I was married. She's my grandmother. I know Ruth is partly Cree, so I don't know if there is a blood relationship, but culturally they were very, very close. So they spent a lot of time together and obviously that's where she got the name from her.

At the time, as an elected leader and being involved with the Women's Shelter, I think the two kind of go hand in hand, one overlaps the other. Ruth being an advocate and protecting the rights of victims, there's no doubt in my mind that the name came from that background. The old lady Bad Boy gave her that name,

Awo Taanaakii, Shield Woman, because what Ruth is doing is a good thing and she's helping out the community. It's a powerful name. Ruth got a very powerful name from an Elder that lived to be 101 years old, and was involved in all the societies. She's like a bishop in our kind of way.

I remember Ruth's Father Tom. I remember him in the smoke ceremonies. I used to see him as one of the Elders that would pray. The smoke ceremonies were for healing. If somebody was sick in the family, they would host a smoke ceremony to pray for that person. I remember Tom, he and my great Grandfather were about the same age. They were part of the Horn Society.

I think in her own time Ruth hit her bottom. There was no other choice but to get on her feet and just become who she is today. When she came to that point in her life, I can't say, but most Aboriginal people, their stories are usually, I ended up in prison, that's where I came to realize that I need to turn my life around, or a spouse died, or they ended up on skid row. I've had a few older friends that said, you know one day my wife and I got up in Central Park in Calgary and said, what are we doing here, we have a home back at Siksika, let's go home, let's clean ourselves up. So different stories, but it's always somebody reaches their rock bottom.

Now, she's been through it all. She survived the holocaust in other words. She shows that resiliency, to say, nothing's going to stop me, I'm going to fight until the day I die. She's got a big heart if you know her, but she's a fierce warrior too if you get on the wrong side of her, and she won't stand down. I've seen her confront Council and former Chiefs, to say, I don't appreciate what you're saying here and I'll have you know. She'll lay down the law and her perspective if she's not in agreement.

Respect. For me I have utmost respect for her because she represents things that mean a lot in life, health, wellness, integrity, honesty, a loving person and helping the needy. She's never afraid to walk amongst them. She'll go to downtown Calgary, the drop-in centre, and go visit with friends there. I'm afraid if I go there, somebody will swing a knife at me, you know most people would think that, but not Ruth, "Oh I'm going to go visit, myself and Margaret Waterchief are going, we're going to help at the drop-in centre." For her it's all about people, it's all about life, its all about healing.

Ruth to me is very sincere. She reminds me of my late Mother, very loving, caring and supportive and always lending a helping hand. She's always helping people out, whether advocating for them to get social assistance, or transportation to their doctor's appointment in Calgary, or to the food bank to get food to last until pay day. It may mean I'm going to drive them up to Calgary and get groceries at the food bank – who does that? Half of the time, I don't have time for my kids cause I'm busy doing something else.

Ruth is a social butterfly. She'll even go up to those people and talk to them, quite often everybody else would be afraid to go near them, they'd say, they're drunk, they're street people. But she'd be right in the middle of them, chatting. She picks up people on the road whether she knows them or not, that's scary stuff you know. Red, white or black, she'll pick them up because it's cold or it's raining or it's getting dark. But you know she picks up hitchhikers and she probably gives them money when she drops them off – here you go, you know, have you had anything to eat?

She's a leader in her own kind of way, in a traditional way, to say, people need to care for these guys, people need to take care of them, people need to advocate for them, because everybody turns a blind eye. She leads from the traditional cultural model, the Medicine Wheel, looking at issues from all sides, the spiritual, the emotional, the mental, and the physical.

She always goes to funerals, paying her last respects and respects to the family that's lost a loved one. She's always at those funerals. When we were on Council, she would ask to be excused because there was a funeral, "They're poor people, they appreciate it when they see leadership at the funerals, they know that we care, so I'm going to go." That was her thought process. She'd say, "You know these poor people, people don't care about them, when they lose loved ones. Niitsitapii... they're human. We need to give them our support, when they see us they feel good that we care about them."

She's a fighter and in a nutshell, she's an absolutely beautiful person. I would have loved, if I had a choice of a Mother, in her modern era, I would have loved to have her as a Mother.

# shared stories: **Olivia and Laura**

Olivia Guy-McCarvill (left) and Laura Lushington are two Mount Royal University students, in the Bachelor of Communications and Journalism Program. In 2012, Laura was in a Women's Studies class when a classmate made her aware of the large number of missing and murdered Aboriginal women in Canada. She was deeply impacted by the issue, and decided to recruit three of her classmates to explore the issue and produce a documentary, that aired on CTV2 in 2013. As part of the process they attended the "Sisters in Spirit" gathering at the Calgary Olympic Plaza, where they saw Ruth Scalp Lock speak on the issue of missing and murdered Aboriginal women. Ruth told me she had been contacted by Olivia after the event, and met with them. I was interested in the views of two young non-Aboriginal women. I spoke with Laura and Olivia at Mount Royal University.

It was a lot of fun talking with Olivia and Laura. They have a high degree of youthful energy and compassion. I was taken with their trepidation of their trip to the Reserve to see Ruth. Olivia's first personal encounter with Ruth is palpable, "whoa."

Listening to their awakening to the issues and to actually walk into the Aboriginal world, meet people, and participate in ceremonies was a view into what is possible between our worlds. I think, for them, it just has to start somewhere. This is how we move beyond "the Other" orientation towards Aboriginal people.

*Laura*: We heard about the Sisters in Spirit event online. I knew about the initiative and I connected this with the missing and murdered women. So we went down and we heard Ruth speak there. We didn't know who she was or anything as we were just beginning our research. We filmed everybody. We didn't know who any of these people were. We were like, "We'll figure that out later guys." There were about 100 people. It was freezing.

*Olivia*: So afterwards Laura and I approached a couple of people to follow up and ask if they could put us in touch with Ruth. After some phone calls back and forth with Ruth we set a day to talk to her about her life and the creation of the Awo Taan Healing Lodge. Ruth was genuinely concerned and wanted to be part of our project. She has a very busy schedule, but she knew the importance of this project and that it could make a difference.

Our partners James and Alli went out to Siksika with us and took some footage. So we went out there – we wanted to talk with generations of people, including Ruth as an Elder.

*Laura*: At Sisters in Spirit, Ruth just kept mentioning all the people she's lost, and she just kept going and going and going and she wouldn't even take a breath. I was like, how, and why? We have to talk to you about this. I wanted to know what her perspective on missing and murdered women and the violence was.

*Olivia*: That's what Laura said she wanted to do when the project started. It was just to give justice to an issue that we felt didn't have enough presence in the media – that was our goal.

*Laura*: For me, personally, I never had any interactions with the Aboriginal community. I didn't know how to approach them, whether they would trust me or if I could trust them. In school, I never had been taught anything about the Aboriginal community in Canada, which is horrible, so I had to do my own research. When I told my parents, they were like "okay, you're going to the reserve, give me the address." I think for a lot of us, it's the "reserve", but I approached it like, they're humans just like us. My intentions are genuine. But still that day I had apprehension, even our profs would tell us, like, four white kids going out to the reserve, you are going to get some strange looks. I think the two communities are misrepresented to each other, and when you first talk to people you're out testing the waters. How quickly can we warm up to each other?

*Olivia*: I've never had to tread so carefully in previous projects like I did in this one. I didn't want to disrespect a culture that was so important to Canadian heritage.

*Laura*: Heading onto the Reserve, we didn't really know where we were going and we said, my gosh, we need to stop and ask for directions. Olivia and I found two guys working on their deck, and we were like, do we ask these guys? So, Alli pulls in and Olivia said, "I'm going to ask," and I said, "Should one of us go by ourselves or should we go together? I'll come with you." They didn't look at us weirdly and they just gave us directions.

So, we found Ruth's office in the Elders Lodge, and we hung out for a while. We went into an empty room, set up the camera and she came.

When she first walked in, she took me off guard. I don't know how to put it. I was expecting her to be more soft, and it was like talking to this other person. Like all of a sudden there was like this big personality and I was like "Whoa! Who is this lady?" She was nicely dressed and well put together and just so sure of herself. She had a presence when she walked in. I was taken aback – Oh my, I was like, this is not what I was expecting. We went into the little room and sat down. We were able to connect right away because we're girls. She asked me, "How do my eyebrows look?"

*Olivia*: She shared a story that a guy told her that eyebrows are the most appealing part of a woman's face. She's very conscious of her own presence. It's right up front, and there's no meandering around

154

it, she's right out there and she's telling you how it is.

*Laura*: Her style really broke the ice for us and let us in. I asked a couple of questions and Olivia conducted the majority of the interview.

*Olivia*: I'm sure she's been trained in some aspect and she's obviously given interviews before. It wasn't like we even needed to mold questions for her. She ran away with her own history. She was compelled by her own story. She just said what she wanted to say. She went into great detail about people she'd lost. What stood out about the story, I think, was how she was affected and how she thinks it's unfair how the rest of her community is also in turn being affected by the violence and loss.

*Laura*: For me, it's her journey of personal growth and self awareness, that she takes the time to think about things that have happened in her life and how they affected her, and how she reacted to them at the time. And I can tell that she goes back and forth in her mind about whether that is how she should have reacted. She self-realizes – she takes time to reflect and to understand what has happened to her – she doesn't close the door on things, she keeps bringing them back and I think that builds her up and builds her personality and her character. You can tell that she really wants to impart those lessons to others – she doesn't want others to go through the same mistakes that she did. I think she understands that people are going to do things, but if she can help them go through the same process of reflection that she has, I think she really thinks that's valuable.

*Olivia*: I guess I got kind of emotional when she started talking about her own struggles with alcoholism and addiction. I got a bit teary and I think I actually cried while I was in the room, because I know what it means to battle your own demons and how it feels to be alone, or if you feel like you have to be alone and use your own strength, to become such a powerful woman. I don't want to say that's what everyone dreams of, but everyone wants to overcome troubles and get to a point in life when they reach their goals.

I guess it's that everybody faces something in their life – to me the most important thing in life is resiliency. The strength that I most admire is resiliency and that's just something that she embodies completely. If there's one word to describe her, I would say it would be resilient. I think that can make you a beautiful person and she's just powerful in her community and as a woman.

*Laura*: Ruth was with her Father and the man that killed her sister had just been released from prison and they ran into him. Ruth's Father noticed that she was getting agitated and was going to go say something to this guy...which I could see Ruth doing. But she told us her Father whispered into her ear, "Forgive him." Obviously he's been through the justice system, there's not much more you can do, just forgive him and the weight will be off your shoulders. For me, that struck me because I have trouble forgiving people for things much less than murder. So that really resonated with me because I hold things in so much and I thought if this lady can, and you can tell she's forgiven him, you can tell she's worked through that. For me to see that in someone was really eye opening, I was, "How do you find it within yourself to do that?"

*Olivia*: Totally. The second she said it you knew, it was in her body language.

*Laura*: But she doesn't just forgive people who put those experiences on her. I think she forgives herself for how she reacted to them – I think that's part of it too. That taught me a lesson too – you can't forgive everybody but yourself. There's no way you're going to be a good person if you get stuck there. She self-actualizes. She is a Buddha. That's interesting because I was in India this summer and a lot of the stuff I saw in the people there I saw in Ruth.

I sat in silence on the way home. We started crying on the way home. I thought, I'm not crying, I'm a hard-ass journalist.

*Olivia*: It was hard to tell our team the story – I didn't know how to explain what had just happened. She's a character. With her presence, you don't really know how to describe it to other people. She just told us tales that really resonated with us and it was hard to reiterate in five minutes what happened. At the time it was very hard to verbalize that experience.

*Laura*: I would say the story is her unrelenting push forward. Ruth will not go backwards. She will not backtrack. She's going to take what she did that day and move forward the next. She's going to keep doing that. She powers through. But it's not careless. It's purposeful. She knows, I don't know how to say this, I think she knows there's a Higher Being out there directing her somewhere and somehow. I think she has a direct line to that and has tapped into that so well that she just pushes through, and she knows that the day after tomorrow is going to be better than the one she just had. She talked about how, when she started working on the shelter idea, people thought she was crazy at first – just to take it on.

*Olivia*: Then a lot of valuable people came along to help, to get to where she wanted it to be. It was definitely a long hard road.

Laura: When I grew up there wasn't anything about Aboriginal history in my textbooks. It was just bits here and there. I hate to say this, but our culture does put Aboriginal people as "the Other." I don't think it's said outright. It's a sublayer.

*Olivia*: It's veiled.

*Laura*: It's hidden...it continues through lack of communication. How are you going to know about each other if you don't talk to each other. That was my biggest thing with this project. I was like, I just want to talk to these people. If I can talk to them and they feel like they can talk to me, I've done my job for the day.

*Olivia*: It was so hard. That's the thing. I think we were pretty successful at going into the Aboriginal community and having them be honest with us. Even if you just scratch the surface, for me at least I felt like we had reached some sort of success. We went into people's homes. We went into very personal spaces to interview people who didn't even know us and I felt like that was already a step in the right direction.

*Laura*: There wasn't one person who when we were done didn't say thank you, you were genuine, I understand what you are doing. Getting beyond the otherness, it's still not happening. I felt bad because I didn't know about the Idle No More rally at Chinook Mall – if I'd known about it I would have been there. I would have joined it, helped out.

*Olivia*: It stems from the very beginning. The hostility has to end. People have to be interested in talking to the people out of pure interest. You can't force that type of thing.

*Laura*: It's even as simple as, in elementary school, having a school unit on the Aboriginal community and having an Elder or representative come in and smudge with the kids. That's as simple as it is. Because you break that barrier, so when there's a rally or something, you're not afraid to go up and say, "Hey, what are you doing, why are you doing this?" I didn't know what smudging was until four months ago. But we went to the Sisters in Spirit and we went to the Justice for Jackie walk and all of a sudden we're smudging with these people. All we did was say, "Hi, how are you?" and you're in. It's not that difficult.

*Olivia*: You're engaged in the ceremonial activities and you're watching them perform traditional dances, and it's beautiful. We were all blown away. I think we picked the best topic. It was astounding.

I've been thinking about how we could do a documentary if we had more time to go out and do a two hour feature. The potential to talk to so many more people is so out there, and just to engage further and keep on doing what we set out to do. But now we're not as naïve and we're more prepared, and we could go in and feel the utmost confidence because we know these people have confidence in us now. I hope.

*Laura*: We have confidence in ourselves I think. For me, now that I have all this information about the Aboriginal community and how to interact with them, I understand the Idle No More movement and I understand a lot of the issues in the Aboriginal community. Even within my own family, they were like, what the heck are you doing, you're nuts, but alright. I'd come home and tell them about my day and what I'd found out, and they still didn't really understand because they weren't smudging with me, they weren't talking to Ruth, they weren't at the Sisters in Spirit or Justice for Jackie Walk. Now I feel like we have almost an obligation to spread this information to more people that we know and to break down those barriers, because as soon as one Caucasian person goes, "Hey, I met a great Aboriginal person today..."

*Olivia*: "...Or hey, I watched a great film that taught me something about them that I hadn't learned about in school..."

*Laura*: or "Hey, I looked at a couple of sections of the Indian Act and this is what happened," or "I read this book, I read Judge John Reilly's book." Like, it doesn't take much, and as soon as you open that door just a little bit you get this flood of information, and suddenly you understand and you become people together.

*Olivia*: I think there's a new story now and Ruth, she's kind of opening people's eyes. That's kind of our mission statement... and I think that's Ruth's mission statement in a way.

# Part VI

# Towards the Future

"We have the power, in our hearts, within ourselves."

# shared stories: **Dana Stonechild**

*Dana is Ruth's Grand Daughter. She is twenty-one years old and lives at Siksika. She speaks quietly and thoughtfully about her Grandmother, her own experience, and the future of her People. She, and the other young people Ruth has influenced is part of her legacy, the next generation.*

One of the main things with my Grandmother is her sobriety. It made her the woman she is today. All the things she has done would not have happened without it. She did it for her family and for herself. Another thing is her humor, she likes to be silly, "Oh, don't be so serious. I'm just joking," she would say. Then there is her compassion. She wants to help people, but not just help, but help people who want to help themselves. Like when she was with leadership, people would ask for spare change, but she would come out with sandwiches and stuff to eat. They would say, "Hey, where's my five dollars?" She wouldn't support their problems, but she is going to feed them, help them in a good way.

My Grandparents basically raised me. I remember when I was three years old, going down to the river with my Grandma and Grandpa, to go pick berries and have picnics with my family. Those are good memories. One time, about ten years ago, there was this really bad storm that lasted about five days. The power was out, and there were a lot of us kids living in the house. Grandma went out into the storm by the house and started a fire, and boiled us meat and potatoes. It was amazing, we were sitting in the dark hungry, and she just pulls it together. I don't know how she started a fire, it was a blizzard. But she did it, she brings it in and she feeds us. I was thinking, that's how she lived as a kid, with her parents. So to her it was peanuts, to go out and do this, prepare a meal for her family. I can still see it.

Being an Aboriginal young person today, it is both good and bad. Now, it is hard, because the new Buffalo is education. That's the way the older people say it. In the past we lived off the Buffalo, as our way of life. Now we have to be educated, to live off of education. So you have to have an education.

There are times I would like to live traditionally, because they say to speak the language, you have to have that mentality. To speak Blackfoot, you have to think Blackfoot. I can speak Blackfoot, but not really fluently. I should be able to, because I was raised by my Grandparents who speak fluent Blackfoot. It's a goal for me. That's where our disadvantage is, right there, us not speaking Blackfoot. If our whole Nation thought like Blackfoot, we wouldn't have these problems, like alcohol and drugs. That would solve a lot of our problems. It's not our way, our way of life, the problems we have today. It's nice to live in the modern world, but as my Uncle told me, "You don't know where you are going to go in this life, until you know where you come from."

Sometimes we don't get treated so well out there in the world. You get looked down upon, because a lot of our young people are suffering from addictions...there is a lot of teen pregnancy.

For the young Aboriginal people today my Grandma represents some important things. Healing has a lot to do with it, and to help shine the spot light on youth. We're not heard, we don't have a voice. With Idle No More for example, I tried to get the leadership involved, but they didn't take me seriously. For Grandma, it is about healing, and helping us find our way, not to get lost in the alcohol and drugs, because for a lot of us, that is our route right now. We're lost, a lot of us on the reserve, and that is her motive, to realize that's not the best road to go down.

With my Grandma, people seek her out, they want to know how she sees things. She is seen as a woman of integrity. You don't have to be shy to ask her to help you, you don't have to beat around the bush. If she can't help you, she will tell you. She will find someone else who can. She will find a way, work around it somehow. Her name, Awo Taanaakii, it means Shield. It was given to her by her Grandma, to protect her from negative things through her life. I guess it worked, because she has had a lot of success in her life. I think that name has served her well. It has served its purpose. She had to earn that name before it was given to her. She has served her Nation for eighteen years on leadership at this point, so now she looks to the Creator to show her what to do next. What she is doing now, with the Family Violence work, that is where she is supposed to be, that is where she is needed.

When I look at Grandma and Theoren Fleury, when he was ready to change his path, he reached out to my Grandma. I find them to be like true friends. They laugh and have fun, because with sobriety for both of them, you have to have humour. I think she has taught him that, just to enjoy life. Their relationship, I find it cute, because he calls them Grandma and Grandpa, and he invites them over to his place. It's just another story where she has helped someone with their sobriety.

My Grandma's roots are important to her. She wants to know more about her background on her mother's side, the Cree side. For her, I want to take her someday to go out to Saskatchewan and meet some of her people. It's something I want to do for her. I have been thinking about this for the last couple of years. It will be hard, because I don't know where the Reserve is, or any of the people. But I guess I will give it a shot. It would be really something. She misses her family, her brothers and sisters. She cries sometimes. So finding family is very important to her.

Grandma has always been my role model from day one, since I knew what a role model was. I looked up to her. She was always so kind and soft spoken when I went to her, for anything. She always knew

164

something was wrong between my Mom, my sister, myself. I would go, "No, nothing is wrong." So we would walk away, and go in our room, but she would get it out of us, someway or the other. She would say, "Just let it out, just cry, don't hold it in." So we would start crying, and she would say, "It's okay, my girl," and we would all be crying and hugging. It just comes to her naturally.

But she can be tough. She is stern. She has values and she always follows through. She always lives by those values. They are strong values about things like honesty, not to lie. If we lied, she would tell us, "Don't tell me that, I know you're lying." Another thing, since I was a little girl it was, "Don't be a follower, be a leader." Where I want to be is not where I am right now. She always had high expectations of me, and sometimes I find it hard to live up to those expectations.

Me, now, I want to experience the college life, then throw it out the window. My best friend is in college now, and I am supposed to be there with her, but at the end of school I got cocky and my marks started to drop and now I am working on my upgrading. Then I want to get into school. I am not sure what I want to do at this point. I want to go down that road of Political Science. I want to go into politics, MLA politics, not just on the Reserve. Like my Grandmother, she made it pretty far, she almost made it onto Provincial politics. It shows that Native people can run in those kind of elections.

She got out there, which is pretty awesome, which is something I want to do. I want to go out there in the big time, roll with the Big Boys. That's where it begins, you can't make a change just being on Council. You can help your people, but when you are up there, you have a better chance of making a change, of being heard. Then there is the Association of First Nations Chief, but to start in some off-Reserve politics. It will be hard, because people will look down on us, because they don't expect us to be there. There probably isn't one of us in there now. We have to get in there, and I want to get in there someway or another. I have a passion for it, and I think I should follow it, and do what I can. I don't want to think five years down the road, I want to think about today and tomorrow, take it day by day. I guess wherever the Creator wants me, he will put me there, and keep me moving forwards...not backwards.

I believe in Our People, not to feud amongst ourselves, but to come together, to be stronger as a Nation. Our ancestors used to come together, because we are a collective people. We have to think about the whole group of people, not just ourselves. So sometimes we have to go back. We have to keep our traditions and our culture, to keep who we are, but we have to move forward too and be part of the modern world.

We are still here, we are still Our People. It will take time for us to change, but it will happen. One day.

Chapter **11** there are problems...but I have hope.

In 1492 when Columbus came, our structure, our culture as a People was in place. We had everything. The way I look at it, invasion came... they discovered and now they're here.

When someone invades your space, that's trauma. Number one, we didn't know the English language and couldn't communicate with them. And they brought alcohol. So right from that time, that's when it all started. Even today, the ripples effect us over generations.

When you experience trauma, intellectually there's certain things that go through the brain. I've been to sessions by psychologists and that's the western way. I understand it, and I respect it. I understand the physical makeup of the brain when we've been traumatized. On the other hand, I used to hear my ancestors say it in Blackfoot – the closest word I can put to it, is frightened or scared: what are these people doing here?

Today, the trauma, it's still there... prejudice, fear, problems. Some just resort to alcohol because they don't know what to do with the trauma. They don't talk to Elders or people in the helping profession. Abuse - when someone invades your space physically, emotionally, or with put downs - when you've been traumatized the trust isn't there anymore. This has to do with my People. I was traumatized at the residential school. Fourteen years is a long time. I was fortunate to have a background where my Father taught me our way. That's how I was able to do something with my drinking, because I already had that foundation.

My people have been traumatized in so many ways over the years. I remember when they filmed our Sundance. "Okan" was the name of the film. You shouldn't take pictures of the Sundance because they're spiritual, it is so sacred, and it takes certain individuals to be members of these Societies. This is like another form of abuse. My Father was a member and he dealt with a lot of stuff in these ceremonies.

They gave us liquor rights in Alberta in the mid 1960's. Then came Child Welfare, all of the children lost to the system. Years ago when you took a child away from their home, they were often lost in the white world. But its different today, they place children with family. Child Welfare has changed quite a bit, which is good, that they consider family to place kids when they're apprehended.

There are times when I really get down. Sometimes I wonder if there is hope with all of the challenges we face daily. It's hard to be a healer, a helper, not just for me but for all people in these roles. We try to help people and then it feels like we take a step back when something bad happens in the community. Very discouraging. You wonder sometimes, will things ever change? I wonder if I should just give up trying to help people and to change our situation. It can be overwhelming. Healing is hard work, very hard and tiring. We're overcoming hundreds of years of history and trauma. The healers and helpers go out daily and try to make a difference, then they go home and face the same problems in their own families. It's so hard. They need outlets to all this, friends, prayer, access to their own healing. Sometimes I have doubt. It can be so tiring. But then I stop, look inside, get in touch with my strength, re-focus, and move on again.

Politically I really feel leadership should look at healing our People, because you have to deal with it. I see so many people on the Nation walking around, they're traumatized -they get picked up, they go to jail and then when they sober up they're all together different. They still have the dignity and respect, but once they start drinking, everything goes. They feel that by drinking everything is going to go away. Maybe temporarily. I can attest to that. I kept covering the trauma, the hurt and pain, but it never got me anywhere, and I can understand that. There should be more healing programs in the First Nations.

I feel that it's important for the leadership to be healthy. What I mean by healthy is that they should be sober because we represent the People and I feel that they should be looking at their own healing. Once I was thinking about it, holy, if I was still a drinker and be in leadership, I don't think I could do the work. You need to lead the people with a sober, clear mind because there's so much to do in leadership. You have to read all these documents and when we have to negotiate with government, you really have to understand the terminology, and be up to par. I have to try and be ahead of them, because there's no consultation with both levels of government. They come up with these documents, something they say is going to better us, but they're always ahead of us.

Consultation is a big concern for me, the way that government has been dealing with First Nations people. If you and I sit down, you have this idea and you're going to present it to me. But you didn't do it. You went to somebody else, without telling me, you're talking to another person or another body. There should be direct communication between the First Nations and the government because with Siksika, the Chief and Council are the government. That's what the Treaty means. You go talk to those people, you don't draft up something and then present it. That's what they've been doing over the years. They talk amongst themselves. They have a Minister of Indian Affairs and then they tell us, this is in place and what do you think of it? It's so ridiculous.

---

We have a lot of good things going now in Siksika. We have this family violence response initiative. We work with the RCMP in a partnership, the first of its kind. We have a very high rate of family and domestic violence and that's why we got this funding from the Province. So we're making headway and we have a relationship with the RCMP and Health. When our People are in a domestic incident, the accused, they take that person to jail. They diffuse the situation and then they ask the other family members, would you like to speak to us, one of the counsellors? So that's how the referrals are made. But the Mom is so happy. Sometimes individuals walk in, they ask us to help them.

We have a mental health program. They have two psychologists. They're working in a traditional way of healing our people. So that's a big step, because right now, some of our people, when you talk to them about it, they don't understand. You have to explain it to them. I explain it in Blackfoot.

Healing is about looking after yourself every day, you get up and you have meals throughout the day and you look after the spiritual part of yourself, making that connection with the Spirits and the Creator. If you're feeling down, you deal with the emotional part, and also if you're physically hurt you deal with that too. Mental health, it has to do with our mind and all the stuff that we've been through. So, we look at the holistic approach. This way they understand mental health, its not that you're crazy and you have to go to a psychologist or mental health therapist, no. This way they understand the importance of healing. When you have a headache, you don't run to your medicine cabinet and grab Tylenol 3's. There's other ways to deal with it, by using the traditional means.

Here, we have a parenting course and there should always be a traditional component, especially for the young girls. If you don't use the traditional component, if you just use the white man's way of parenting, it's not going to work. We have to teach these young women parenting, how it used to be years ago. It's very basic, even just how we look at mothering and children. Let's say a young woman, she's pregnant, she goes to a wake or a funeral. Back in the day, you couldn't do it, you always cover yourself with a shawl or even a jacket.  Back in those days, they really looked after themselves, and women were very sacred, especially when they're carrying a baby. So that, I see is lacking.

Today, I look at all this violence.  In a relationship, you both have something to contribute or to say in that relationship. Men and women, they need to respect one another. Even our young women can be aggressive today. So we all have to look at ourselves. I've been through it when I was drinking. It all took time. The training we do in the family violence program, we're teaching them to be assertive, to say her part to her partner. We're going to be offering more courses for the men, how to communicate and treat their wives with that respect.

I was talking with one of our Judges recently, and he said Ruth, you're always in here. He said it's so important, because people really respect Elders. I told him I come because I want to support the People, the youth especially.  My clients say, "Ruth, can you come to court, I'm so scared and I feel good when you're there." They sit with me in the courtroom and it's good because I have a relationship with the Judge, who speaks Blackfoot. Sometimes if I have to help someone in court, he asks me to come up to the Bench. One time I was talking to the Judge, and I said, "Your Honor," and he was just smiling, but you have to respect his role. We Indians, we have so much humor, and he said, "Ruth, why don't you just speak in Blackfoot to me?"

My hope for the youth is for them to learn the language, to learn their culture, everything, to learn the clan system. Like my granddaughter, yesterday I introduced Dana to a cousin, and I told Dana, they're related, and I explained how you're related. He was so thankful, "Dana I'm so glad to meet you and to know that we're related. Grandma, thank you for telling me."  This way in the community, they know each other, and it just takes a few minutes to explain it to them. So the Elders really have to help them.

My number one concern is the drinking and the drugs, and I think there's hard drugs on the Reserve. We have to, I don't like to say, save their lives, but I guess in some ways that's what I mean. We have to find a way to do something, to take them away from all the alcohol and drugs and put them on a different road. We can do that. It's possible. These programs we have, our traditional way should be in there - the clan system, parenting, language and culture. Also really look at the recreation department. We need to really evaluate all these programs, including when they are open. All of this takes resources and support.

It would be good it we were a dry reserve, not to bring liquor onto the reserve, to charge them if they bring liquor. But I guess in a way we cannot control them, but at least if we have something, our people will think, okay, if I go home and I get stopped, or somebody will call the police if they see all this liquor. You can do it – it takes a Band Council Resolution.

Back in the day, I didn't start drinking until I was 19. I was in the school, but during summer holidays or whenever I didn't drink. I was kept at home, I was sheltered, I never had a boyfriend, never went on a date. It was a good thing, because my Mother and Father were so strict with me.

---

I have two children. My daughter Karleen has three children, and my son Trevor has three children. I have many step children – my husband Francis has six children, and I have numerous Grandchildren and adopted Grandchildren.

When I had my children, I didn't really have parenting skills. I didn't really have the slightest idea when I had my children because at the Residential School we weren't taught about parenting. I didn't have anybody like a mentor, a woman, or an older woman to teach me – I had to learn the hard way. It was really tough. My late sister, Lucy Crane Bear wanted to adopt my daughter Karleen. Then she was murdered, so I really had a hard time.

My Father, Tom Scalp Lock, really helped me out. He helped me out financially to raise my children. He always made sure we had food, and that the kids were taken care of. He gave me money every month to help me out and I just learned along the way. Then there was this Elder from Tsuu T'ina, she used to come and babysit because I always had to have a job. I had so much anger at the time. I always... I don't like to say abused...just how I raised my children. It was just like the attitude I got from the Residential School, sometimes I was too harsh with them, and my Father used to tell me, "You're going to have to change your tone, your attitude – this is like a reform school the way you treat your kids." My father told me, how you treat your kids, they're going to have so much resentment towards you as a mother, because I didn't know how to parent, I didn't know about being a Mother. I never hugged my children, like even to tell them, "Oh I love you," or "I'm sorry I spanked you or got after you." Everything had to be just-so – you can't come into the house with muddy feed, this and that. My house was always clean, you could eat off the floor because that's how I was raised at the Residential School.

If I were to go back, what I know today, to raise my children...it seems today, my children and especially my great Grandchildren, I have so much more patience. I enjoy working with my great grandchildren, like their homework, sitting down to talk to them in a caring manner. It took me a long time to come to terms with what I went through. I look at the way I was brought up by my parents, to always make sure to have food on the table, to work hard to raise your children. These children are your responsibility, you brought them into this world, regardless of what you're going through. I always made promises to my children when I was drinking and I never followed through. But things changed over the years – like how I feel about being a parent today. I was the lousiest Mother years ago. Sure I kept my kids clean, did a lot of laundry, and whatnot, but I was too harsh. I should have softened up I guess. It took me a long time to deal with it... to heal. I always remember what I learned from my parents, my Mother, to have a name for your child and follow through with that, to look at children as gifts from the Creator.

My relationship with my children now, it's really good. My Son shows a lot of respect and appreciation. He knew that we had such a hard time. We had nothing. My daughter, Karleen, she remembers the time when she was a little girl and we couldn't even afford her birthday that year, so what did Bob Hawkesworth do? He brought two boxes of cake mix. The two boxes were to make Karleen a birthday cake. That's how poor we were. That's how come today I really appreciate what I have, because back then, I didn't have anything for my kids and it was always second hand stuff. Bob, he really did a lot of good things for us. At Christmas, we always picked up the Indian people living in Calgary, we had a big turkey dinner, we had a potluck and it was so good for me because I was able to afford something to contribute to the potluck. Bob organized it and we did the work together.

Time and time again, I've talked to the children about my life. I've also written to the children. If I've hurt their feelings, if I've hurt them in any way, please forgive me. I always ask for forgiveness. These are my personal convictions. If they're going to follow my path, I'll be so happy. I've built this road for them, I can lead them to water, but I cannot make them drink. So, it's up to them. My children, step-children, adopted children, they have children, and they can only show them there's a good way, without alcohol, because that's our big problem.

I want to tell my grandchildren, they have to forgive. They have to forgive their parents that they separated, and they cannot keep on hating, or don't like their parents. You have to forgive your parents that they didn't raise you the way they should – they had their own problems and you have to let go of those bad feelings. There's nothing you can do about the past, you have to accept it. You have to do something about it, because if you don't forgive, it's you that's hurting, not that person. You can't keep on carrying that baggage around. Who are we not to forgive?

I talk to the children because it's going to be tough. We're at a crossroads for Native people right now, politically. One of my Grandchildren couldn't even get sponsorship to go to post-secondary. What are we going to do? That's when I tell them everything that I've done. I use to go work for these rich people in Calgary and they gave me food, clothes and they paid my bus fare. I had to do something because I didn't want to see my kids starve. It was hard living on welfare because it was for the rent, the basic needs. So I always tell my children about what I went through. I don't hide anything, even my drinking. I tell them, you people have to understand, I never had anything on a silver platter.

So, sometimes I get after them, to get off their fanny and do something. They get mad, maybe it's how I come across. I get after my grandchildren. Maybe I am too harsh, but certain behaviours I don't like. You're on the cell phone all hours of the night, "Okay, get off that phone." They used to call me Hitler! My grandchildren, or my nephews, they say, "Oh, you went to the old school." But I always tell them, "If I don't talk to you, it means I don't care." You have to talk to them. I even tell that to my Grandchildren, "Grandma won't be here forever, you have to learn, to continue and always remember my legacy and what I taught you."

"Today, I'm so thankful that you grandchildren never saw me drunk, that I'm sober now," I told this to my Grandson. We were driving down the road one day and this elderly man was picking up bottles to take to the bottle depot. My Grandson looked at me and I knew something hit him. We were going to Strathmore and I told him, how did you feel about that man picking up bottles, and he said, "I can't imagine, and you Grandma you're old and for you to be picking up bottles..." and I told him "If I hadn't quit drinking I'd probably be doing the same, picking up bottles, take them to the liquor store, and get drunk." But I told him, "I did that many years ago, but you didn't see me..."

Now's the time for our children to do something with their life. The way things are going, maybe in the future we won't even have funding for education and social assistance. I want them to get somewhere, don't be lazy, get up in the morning. My Uncle Alex always told me you have to get up in the morning, there was no such thing as Indian time, and that's why they were so offended. I was taught, get up in the morning, you'll get things done, don't lose out on the good things of life, stay active, be ahead of the game. I was proud of that way. The first thing in the morning, at the break of dawn, my Father used to go out and pray and it was so important. I even go out, just once in a long while, just to appreciate the morning. There's a name in our culture for the break of day and when you pray, it's the most powerful time of the day. I thank the Creator that I woke up sober. I was taught all these different things. I really had to go back in my healing. My parents, what they taught me, and even recently, some more stuff surfaced from the way I was raised... the good things.

---

I want to see some things different in the future. I see all of these dogs running around, they're starving, and it really bothers me. I don't want to see dogs on the reserve starving. I want animals to be looked after. I don't want horses running around along the ditches and in the townsites. We lost a lot of our ways, to look after these animals, because they have feelings too. I want our Reserve to be garbage free. What I mean by that, it really bothers me when I see garbage in the ditches, all over the townsite. We need to take care of our stuff. We can't damage, let's say, that Arbor down the hill, or the Sportsplex. When you start your healing, you want to look good on the inside, but you want to look good on the outside, your home, too. That's why my husband he put up that fence, and he said, "This is our haven." A lot of people give us compliments, people that come in the Summer. Our yard is beautiful, flowers, and we continue growing trees.

Even the inside of your home has a lot to do with you as a person. I was always taught, if you don't have groceries in the house, that's not a home. So when I get paid, what I do, I go to shop for groceries. That's the number one. Make it a home, kids need to eat. A lot of

176

the times when our People get welfare, they go to town, they just buy little bags of food. How is that little bag of food going to last all month? So we have to teach them things like budgeting, or if there's a way they could go to the No Frills store and stock up on food for the month, because a lot of them don't have food.

Mostly, I want our people to be healthy.

If I look twenty years in the future, I want to really clean up the reserve, to be alcohol free, drug free, violence free and for our young people to have a really good education, both the white way and the Indian way. Just to be a positive, healthy Nation.
We have to get going and quit blaming, "Oh, the government this and that..." With me, I look at the good side, because I lived on the outside for so many years. I adopted a lot of the ways from the white people and I kept the good things I learned from the Residential School. I add those things to being an Indian woman, a Blackfoot woman, and the things I learned from my parents. I really used all these different skills.

In twenty years, I would like to see all people understand each other, where they're coming from. I would like if non-Aboriginal people could understand why we're like this today, the drinking, all these social problems, being violent. Twenty years is a long time from now and hopefully we get to educate all walks of life and vice versa so we all understand where we're coming from. It can happen. Everything is possible. It will take commitment and people to participate in different gatherings. Come down with some of your friends to Siksika and participate in the different things that we do on the Nation. Then more people will be coming and understand and experience the Sundance, just to be there. Not just pow wows, they are more social. It's good to come to the powwows too, but all kinds of different things.

I would like to see in the mainstream education system and in university curriculum, more education on Siksika and other First Nations. When you're young, you're not prejudiced. These young people, they're open to learn. There were two students that came to interview me. They were non-Native. They were even crying because of what I was sharing with them. They were interested in the Shelter and why it started and why we have so many problems. Of course, I was crying and they said they never spoke to an Indian person before. These kind of conversations are important. We're responsible, too, to share our ways with people on the outside, but they should really educate at colleges and universities. There's a lot of things that they can learn from us, and we're always interested in other people, not just the white people.

I always pray that in the future our youth will have a good life. We have to help them get out of that, I don't want to say black hole or rut, but where they're at, to put them on the right road. I pray that they will live a healthy lifestyle, free from drugs, to have an education, to be traditional and to respect people, especially the Elders.

I have reason to be optimistic about some things happening in the Aboriginal community in Canada. In 2012, the Canadian Government tried to pass Legislation that our People felt affected our Treaty rights, and non-Aboriginal people as a whole. We don't think it was done openly. We weren't consulted because it seems like the Government doesn't want to talk to and listen to our leaders. People rose up. This helped create the Idle No More movement across Canada. I think who is driving this is younger people, people with an education, who understand what the issues are. They are vocal and want to be a part of what is happening. It is the youth who will be in the forefront of positive change. At their age, I was not as aware of the issues as they are, understanding funding arrangements, and how things were working. And it is young women. Women, traditionally, have always been a part of our leadership. They want to be involved in what is happening, and they are educating their peers, and getting non-Aboriginal people involved. Look how people came out to support us, coming to Round Dances in shopping malls. These people had momentum, and knew how to organize things. They are very committed, marching, socializing together, and on the internet. They know we need a plan, a plan for the future. One thing I do not support is any form of violence to achieve our goals. This does not help. It only continues the cycle, and breaks relationships.

We need to work together, to work hard. We have to advocate for resources, in education and health, so we can be a healthy people, and move ahead. And we have to work hard ourselves, like my parents' generation. They worked so hard, on the farm, in jobs, in the coal mines. This was before welfare, before liquor rights, all of which just took our pride. I know lots of people who never drank until we got these rights. When they hunted, it was shared.

On one hand, there are many problems that sometimes feels overwhelming. There are powerful, negative influences on our youth, the music, the dress, violence in the media, Facebook. On the other hand, we have our hope and our growing awareness, and educated young people. So we have to work hard to heal, to overcome the past, and make a brighter future. Our healers bring knowledge and an alternative to all the negative influences.

It is important to keep moving, to keep growing. Even me, at my age, I still want to learn and contribute. So, even though I didn't have a college education when I was young, I have finished the Indigenous Leadership and Management Program at the Banff Center. I did it one course at a time. It took me many years. I don't know how I will use it, but I will, somehow. I am now working front - line in domestic violence in my community, working shifts. That is what makes me feel good, being on the ground, helping people any way I can.

---

Our people have a purpose. We can conquer anything. We have the power, within ourselves. We have the history. Many of our people brought us to where we are today – we have the tools. We could be thriving.

It is a beautiful life, and I am not worried. Always something will come along.

Life is fragile, let's enjoy what we have. But there is much to do. Now it is time that we need to find a different way, a healthy way, balanced, not in anger.

We need to be forgiving, first forgive yourself. We need to pray to the Creator, all of us, as a community. Pray for the abusers, and the victims, of all colors. We need to live in the Medicine Wheel, in the four quadrants, physical, mental, spiritual, and emotional.

People feel shame in being an Indian. Our children need a sense of belonging, of where they came from. It is my purpose to be a storyteller, to help our young people to understand our history, of who we are. In the end I want to give...I don't ask for anything in return.

When I look back now, it has been a long and hard road. So much has happened in my life. I remember as a young child, my Father and my Mother, my brothers and my sisters. I learned so much from all of them. When I hear the songs and the drums today, I remember the old, holy songs. I remember the confusion and being lost in the years at school, then the years of drinking, my spirit gone... finding myself again through the Creator. The healing work, myself, others, the community. My name, Awo Taanaakii, the spirit power of the Shield. All the work in making the Shelter happen, the years as elected leadership on my Nation. All the people I have met, my special friends in my life who will stay until the end, and those who have harmed me, but I forgive. So much has happened. One day, I will see my Grandfather again, and honour him. I will take my Mother back to the place she came from, that I couldn't do in this life.

Thank you my friends, for listening to my story. I hope you will have learned something about my People and our experience. I hope we have a better understanding of each other, and a brighter future, all of us together.

I pray for my People. I pray for you, your families, and for all People.

Ruth and Jim would like to thank a lot of people. Special thanks to Theoren Fleury, Bob Hawkesworth, June Wiggins, Mary Jane Amey, Nelson Gutnick, Leroy Wolf Collar, Olivia McCarvill-Guy, Laura Lushington, and Mildred Broad Scalplock. This is your story too.

Jim would like to thank some people who made this project possible. First, Ruth, thanks for being my friend and letting me in on your story. It has been amazing, "for sure!" Gord Cummings, thanks for your stories, amazing support and editing. Thanks to Sheena, my daughter, awesome editor who kept me laughing with her notes! Thanks to Colleen Biondi, super advice, editing, and encouragement, and thanks to my sister Vicki. Thanks to Casey Eagle Speaker for translations, and Mike Lickers for "the Gift." You all helped us make it happen. Mostly, thanks to the Creator, who gave us the spirit to share this story, persevere, and hopefully, do a little bit for the future of "all our relations."

67717436R00123

Made in the USA
Charleston, SC
20 February 2017